'hoto by Marceau

DEFENSELESS AMERICA

BY

HUDSON MAXIM

*" The quick-firing gun is the greatest
life-saving instrument ever invented."*
Page 83.

HEARST'S INTERNATIONAL LIBRARY CO.
NEW YORK

FOREWORD

***

THIS BOOK IS PRESENTED

WITH THE

COMPLIMENTS OF THE AUTHOR

To a Few Selected Leaders of American Thought
and Shapers of Public Opinion

***

DEAR READER:

I send you this book in the hope that if not already convinced, you will be convinced by it of the defenseless state of this country—convinced that our danger is as great as our weakness. I hope that you may be moved to use your influence that this country may, by adequate preparation against war, safeguard the property, honor and lives of its people and the sanctity of the American home from violation by a foreign foe.

If you are already convinced of our great need then the reading of this book may still strengthen your conviction and stimulate your efforts in the cause of national defense.

FOREWORD

After you have read the book, kindly lend it to your friends, that they also may read it.

Defenseless America was published a year ago at two dollars per copy. Several editions of the book have already been printed and sold.

Soon after the publication of the work I presented ten thousand copies, with my compliments, to students graduating in American universities. This has given many persons the impression that Defenseless America is a book for free distribution.

To correct such an impression, let me say most emphatically that this book is not free, except to a few persons whom I have selected, and to whom I have sent it free at my own personal expense, for the good of the cause of national defense.

The book has exerted so marked an influence in rousing the people of this country to their needs for defense against the red hell of war, that the publishers, through patriotic duty, have placed the good it is doing above all considerations of profit to themselves, and have supplied me copies of this edition of the work absolutely at cost.

The publishers have also put an edition of the book on sale, of which this copy is a specimen, at only fifty cents a copy. In order to enable them to do this, I have cut out all royalties on sales which they may make.

FOREWORD

This edition of the book may be bought of or ordered through any book store at fifty cents a copy, or from the publishers, Hearst's International Library Company, 119 West 40th Street, New York, N. Y., who will send single copies of the book to any address on receipt of sixty cents, or they will send ten copies of the book, in a single package, to any address on receipt of five dollars—fifty cents a copy.

Copies of the regular library edition, printed on superior paper and bound in extra cloth, gold stamping, may be obtained from booksellers or direct from the publishers at two dollars a copy.

Many of the readers of this book have already seen that wonderful motion picture play, "The Battle Cry of Peace," founded upon it.

Commodore J. Stuart Blackton, President of the Vitagraph Company of America, who wrote the scenario of "The Battle Cry of Peace", has this to say about Defenseless America:—

"To the fearless patriotism of Hudson Maxim and the plain, practical, straightforward truths in his book, 'Defenseless America,' I owe the inspiration and impetus which caused me to conceive and write the scenario of 'The Battle Cry of Peace.'

"The object of both book and picture is to arouse in the heart of every American citizen a sense of his strict accountability to his government in time of need, and to bring to

the notice of the greatest number of people
in the shortest possible time the fact that
there is a way to insure that peace for which
we all so earnestly pray.''

Commodore Blackton, being a staunch patriot
and a man with phenomenal vision and breadth of
understanding, and being one of the largest pro-
ducers of motion pictures in the world, saw at
once, as soon as he read Defenseless America,
that the best way to impress the American people
with the message of the book, as he had himself
been impressed by reading it, was to visualize
that message in a great motion picture. Then the
people would be able to see, with their own eyes,
those terrible things happening in our country
and in our very homes, which are happening
abroad and which are surely going to happen to
us if we do not prepare, and immediately and
adequately prepare to save the country.

Faithfully yours,

HUDSON MAXIM.

MAXIM PARK,
LANDING P. O.,
NEW JERSEY,
1916

PREFACE

THE main object of this book is to present a phalanx of facts upon the subject of the defenseless condition of this country, and to show what must be done, and done quickly, in order to avert the most dire calamity that can fall upon a people—that of merciless invasion by a foreign foe, with the horrors of which no pestilence can be compared.

We should bring a lesser calamity upon ourselves by abolishing our quarantine system against the importation of deadly disease and inviting a visitation like the great London Plague, or by letting in the Black Death to sweep our country as it swept Europe in the Middle Ages, than by neglecting our quarantine against war, as we are neglecting it, thereby inviting the pestilence of invasion.

Self-preservation is the first law of Nature, and this law applies to nations exactly as it applies to individuals. Our American Republic cannot survive unless it obeys the law of survival, which all individuals must obey, which all nations must obey, and which all other nations are obeying. No individual, and no nation, has ever disobeyed that law for long and lived; and it is too big a task for the United States of America.

It is the aim of this work to discover truth to the reader, unvarnished and unembellished, and, at the same time, as far as possible, to avoid personalities. Wherever practicable, philosophic generalizations have been tied down to actualities, based upon experiential knowledge and innate common-sense of the eternal fitness of things.

The strong appeal of Lord Roberts for the British nation to prepare for the Armageddon that is now on, which he knew was coming, did not awaken England, but served rather to rouse Germany.

Admiral Mahan pleaded long with his country for an adequate navy. All the Great Powers of the world except America were stimulated by his logic to strengthen their navies. The beautiful, imaginative, logical language of General Homer Lea, on America's military weakness, in his "Valor of Ignorance" and "The Day of the Saxon," has caused many a gun to be made, many a battalion of troops to be enlisted, and many a warship to be built—in foreign countries.

The eloquent words of wisdom of Lord Roberts, Admiral Mahan, Homer Lea, and all real friends of peace and advocates of the only way of maintaining peace—by being prepared against war— have fallen on a deaf America. I am well aware of the fact that nothing I can say will rouse the people of my country to the reality and magnitude of their danger, and to a true appreciation of the imperative necessity for immediate preparation against war.

Possibly this book may lessen a little the effect of the pernicious propagandism of the pacifists—may somewhat help Congressional appropriations for defense—may place a few more men and a few more guns on the firing-line, and thereby save the lives of a few of our people—may save a few homes from the torch—may lessen the area of devastation—may, by adding a little power to our resistance, help to get slightly better terms from the conquerors for our liberation.

Pacifism has ringed the nose of the American people and is leading them, blind and unknowing, to the slaughter. War is inevitable. It matters not that, if this country could be roused, it might be saved. When it is impossible to vitalize the impulse necessary to the accomplishment of a thing, that thing is impossible. So, I say, war is inevitable and imminent.

The American people could not now be roused sufficiently to avert the impending calamity even by a call that would rift the sky and shake down the stars from heaven!

Fate has decreed that our pride shall be humbled, and that we shall be bowed to the dirt. We must first put on sackcloth, ashed in the embers of our burning homes. Perhaps, when we build anew on the fire-blackened desolation, our mood may be receptive of the knowledge that we must shield our homes with blood and brawn and iron.

HUDSON MAXIM.

Maxim Park,
    Landing P. O.,
        New Jersey.
           March, 1915.

CONTENTS

ILLUSTRATIONS

INTRODUCTION

OUR GREAT OBSESSION

SUCCESS in every human pursuit depends upon ability to discern the truth and to utilize it. Facts, though they may be stern, are our best friends, and we should always welcome them with an open mind.

Napoleon said that with good news there is never any hurry, but with bad news not a moment is to be lost. Consequently, those who discover to us certain facts of serious concern are our friends, even though it may be bad news. It is every man's duty, not only to himself, but also to those dear to him, to know the truth about anything which may menace his and their welfare, in order that he and they may become awakened to the danger and prepare for it accordingly.

Those who deceive us by warning us of danger when there is no danger may not do us any harm; in fact, they may even do us good by cultivating our alertness and awareness. The hare may jump at a thousand false alarms to every one of actual danger; but it is the false alarms that have given him the alertness to save himself when real danger comes. On the other hand, those who convince us that there is no danger when there is great danger are the worst of enemies; they expose us, naked of defense, to the armed and armored enemy.

Among the great deceivers with whom the human race has to contend is the confidence man, for he plays upon the fears, vanity, and credulity of his victim with the skill of a Kubelik upon the violin. He enlists his victim with him, and they work together to the same end. No man is greatly deceived by another except through his own cooperation. Every one has his pet egoistic illusion always under the spotlight of self-view; to him, his own importance is a veritable obsession.

A nation is only a compound of individuals, and what is true of an individual also holds true of any aggregation of individuals.

We, the people of the United States of America, are at this moment, and have been for many years, afflicted with a dominating egoistic obsession concerning our greatness, our importance, and our power, while we correspondingly underrate the greatness, the importance, and the power of other nations and races. Our accomplishments have indeed been marvelous, and we have not neglected to award them all the marveling that is their due.

There is no denying the fact that in many competitive pursuits requiring intellectual acuteness for the greatening of material welfare we have outstripped the rest of the world. But the rest of the world has been busy, too, and though we may possibly deserve more credit for our accomplishments in the aggregate than any other people, still, others have far outdone us in many important respects.

Our hitherto isolated and unassailable geographical position has enabled us to utilize our unequaled resources to become the greatest industrial and the wealthiest people in the world.

We have not been obliged to concern ourselves very much thus far with measures for national security, and having at home all the land we needed, we have acquired the habit of looking upon national armaments in the light of frills, which we must maintain merely for national respectability. Many of us look upon our Navy as dress-parade paraphernalia, to be worn on gala occasions.

Our response to the advocacy of a sufficient navy, of coast fortifications, and of a standing army adequate to our needs, has been that we have no use for either army or navy, and that coast fortifications would be a useless expense.

Our enormous wealth and inexhaustible resources have been and still are pointed out as reasons why we require no armaments, although, as a matter of fact, they are the strongest possible reasons for armaments of a magnitude proportionate to that wealth and those resources.

In America, we pride ourselves upon our so-called free institutions, blindly believing that they are free, and that, therefore, every man being an aristocrat, we, by consequence, have no aristocracy, entirely oblivious to the fact that we have merely substituted the esteem of wealth, and the power and the privilege which it represents, for the esteem of family worth and family name, and the power and the privilege which they represent.

Isolation and wealth beget vanity and arrogance; and vanity, resting upon the laurels of past accomplishments, rapidly fosters decadence and weakness; so that the very pride of strength and virility begets weakness and effeminacy.

It has been said that usually there are but three generations between shirt-sleeves and shirt-sleeves. The old man trades upon the name made in the days of his younger strength, and the son, seldom possessing the strength of the father, trades on the father's name, while the third generation generally gets back to shirt-sleeves again. Although this statement is not a general truth, it has truth enough to excuse it.

The main reason why luxury and opulence lead to degeneracy, weakness, and effeminacy, is that those who live on Easy Street, being relieved of the intense strife necessary to gain a livelihood and to climb to positions of opulence and power, suffer from weakness and decay, and finally find their way down to shirt-sleeves, at the foot of the economic and social ladder, either to be submerged in hoboism, or to make the climb of old progenitors over again.

What is true of individuals and families in this respect holds true also of nations, only it takes a little longer time, starting from shirt-sleeves, to get back to shirt-sleeves again.

We Americans were taught by the promoters of the American Revolution—in short, by the fathers of our country—that all men are created equal in respect to privilege, and that no class distinction and no class privilege were worthy of honor unless earned. By consequence, the symbol and the badge of our class distinction became the dollar.

Taught to despise aristocracy, we immediately created for ourselves a new aristocracy in the shape of a plutocracy. This aristocracy of wealth was fast becoming as tyrannical and unbearable and as much a menace to the freedom of the people as the old aristocracy which it had replaced. The old aristocracy had been established by the right of the sword; the new aristocracy had been established by the purchasing power of the dollar, and the people learned that combinations of wealth were a compelling power as great as the combination of armies, and that a government dominated by the dollar might become as intolerable as any form of absolutism.

Then there came another American revolution, led by the labor unions, which proved that it is only necessary for the people to organize, in order to conquer with the short-sword of the ballot as effectually as with the sword of steel.

Unhappily, just as intolerance and avarice have always led conquerors to be overgrasping and tyrannical, so have intolerance and avarice made prosecutions under the Sherman Law veritable persecutions. Now that the common people have found their power, nothing under heaven can halt them, or prevent them from abusing that power, except a higher education of the common people and their leaders, compelling them to understand the great truth that the people of a nation must co-operate with a patriotism that shall emulate the spirit of the hive of bees so admirably interpreted by Maeterlinck.

Nevertheless, we must remember that, while we may with advantage imitate the bee in this respect, the bee does not progress. There has been no enlightenment in bee-life for a hundred thousand years, for the very reason that the bees are dominated by that beautiful spirit of the hive.

We owe our ability to progress and to become more and more highly intelligent and enlightened, to the existence of that instability and heterogeneity which stimulate and develop us by causing us to strive for stability and homogeneity.

Life is a series of reactions between the individual and environing stimuli. For this reason, stern and exacting stimuli are required to develop a man to the full. In all the ages during which the race has been developing there have existed formative influences of the sternest and most exacting kind; so that, just as our ears are constituted to hear only a certain character of sounds, and sounds of a limited pitch, duration, and loudness, and are deaf to all other sounds, so are we constituted to react only to certain environing stimuli, and to react with each stimulus in a certain definite measure, and only in a certain definite measure. It is impossible for us to react supremely, or to be developed supremely, by mediocre stimuli, but we must have supreme stimuli, and in order to get those stimuli, there must be a prompting to activity that demands of a man every ounce of his strength; and everything that is dear to him must be staked to bring out and develop all the latent, larger energies that are in him.

Nothing that can be said and done by all the friends of national defense will make this country take adequate measures for its defense. Nothing but a disastrous war will supply the necessary stimulus. In all the history of the world, this truth has been made manifest—that no nation can be made adequately to prepare against war, no matter what the menace may be, without either suffering actual defeat, or being so embroiled in war as to realize the necessity for preparedness.

INTRODUCTION

This country must first be whipped in order to prepare sufficiently to prevent being whipped. Therefore, our business at the present time is to pick our conquerors. I choose England. I would much rather see the red-coat in the streets of New York than the spiked helmet. I would much rather see the genial face of the British Tommy Atkins than the stern mystery of the Japanese face.

If England does not give us a good, timely whipping, we are going to be whipped by Germany or Japan, and the humiliation will be more than is really needed to stimulate us for adequate preparation.

When the present war is over, the precipitation of a war with England may not depend on what England will choose to do, but it may depend on what we shall choose to do. We have been a lamb rampant for a long time in a jungle alive with lions, and we have owed our security to the fact that the lions have been watching one another, and have not dared to avert their eyes long enough to devour us. If we did not have a grandiose sense of our importance and power, we should not need a whipping in order to prepare against war, but so long as we believe that we can beat all creation without any preparation, we are going to act just as though it were true, and England, although she may be friendly, may be forced, by our inconsiderate bluff and arrogance, to declare war on us. Much better England than any other country. England now has no territorial aspirations that would make her want to annex some of our land. She would be satisfied with a good big indemnity, which we could well afford to pay for the benefit we should gain from the war. If England will merely come over seas, and whip us, and tax us for the trouble, and thereby lead us to prepare adequately to defend ourselves against less friendly nations, she will do us the greatest possible good.

We are living and working not alone for ourselves, but also for those who are our own, and for all others insomuch as their interests and their welfare are in common with our own.

Our welfare is part and parcel of the aggregate welfare of all those for whom we are working, and our welfare and their welfare are not only a condition of the present, but are also a condition of the future. The welfare of our children and our children's children, and of those whose interests will be in common with theirs, is part and parcel of our own present welfare. This is the true philosophy by which we who are sane and conscientious are guided. Upon such philosophy are based all economics and all prudence.

The false philosophy of the selfish and the sensual, the spendthrift and the debauchee, is the philosophy of such as they whose acts of omission and commission brought on the French Revolution, and who said, *"Après nous le déluge";* but such should not be our philosophy.

Therefore, if now there be a calamity in the making, which we are able to foresee must surely descend upon the heads of our children, even if it does not come soon enough to fall upon our own heads, it is a thing that should awaken our concern and stimulate our inquiry, and lead us to seek ways and means for averting it.

It is a fact, which I absolutely know as certainly as anything can be known in human affairs, that we, and all of those who are near and dear to us, are sitting today on a powder magazine with the train lighted, and it is only a question of the slowness, or quickness, of the fuse when the time shall arrive for the explosion.

The laws that govern human events are as mathematically accurate and as immutable as the laws that govern the motions of the heavenly bodies; the laws that govern human reactions—the reactions between men and men, communities and communities, nations and nations—are as immutable and are governed as exactly by the laws of cause and effect as are chemical reactions. Nothing can happen without a cause, and there can be no cause that does not make something happen. Every event is the child of its parents—cause and effect.

Now let us look at the parentage of the cause and effect whose progeny are soon to bring upon us the great red peril of war, and, finding us unprepared, will treat us as Germany has treated Belgium. We are rich—our country from one end to the other possesses a vast wealth of enticements to the invasion of a foreign foe—and we are defenseless. These conditions are the parents of vast impending calamities.

Europe, today, is involved in the greatest war in the history of mankind, and—in spite of all the saving grace of our so-called modern civilization, in spite of all the mercifulness of the Christian religion, in spite of all the charitable kindness of the Red Cross—the sum of brutality, savagery, and misery of this war is certainly not much less than it has been at any other time in the history of a striving world, every page of which has been written with blood.

We have arrived at a time when we must decide whether or not our safety can be better secured and peace maintained with armaments or without armaments.

DEFENSELESS AMERICA

DEFENSELESS AMERICA

CHAPTER I

DANGEROUS PREACHMENTS

"There will be no war in the future, for it has become impossible now that it is clear that war means suicide."
I. S. Bloch, "The Future of War," 1899.

"What shall we say of the Great War of Europe ever threatening, ever impending, and which never comes? We shall say that it will never come. Humanly speaking, it is impossible."
Dr. David Starr Jordan, "War and Waste," 1913.

THEY who are loudest in their vociferations about the calamities that the warring nations of Europe have brought upon themselves are those peace-palavering persons who have been telling us all along, during the past twenty-five years, that human nature had improved so much lately, and the spirit of international brotherhood had become so dominant, that the fighting spirit was nearly dead in the souls of men.

The peace praters have assured us from time to time that the last great war of the world had been fought; they have told us that no great nations would dare to go to war any more, because war between any of the Great Powers would now mean bankruptcy and national suicide; they have assured us that all international differences would hereafter be settled by jurisprudential procedure, and that law would be substituted for war.

About fifteen years ago, a M. de Bloch " proved " in his book, entitled " The Future of War. Is War Now Possible? " that war had become so deadly and destructive, and, above all, so expensive, as to be impossible. So impressed was the Czar of Russia with de Bloch's arguments that he called a conference of the nations to consider disarmament. Since that time a thousand different persons have, in a thousand different ways, " proved " to us that war on a large scale was not only impossible, but also absolutely unthinkable. Droll, isn't it, that the nations keep right on fighting? We are consoled, however, by the insistence of the peace prophets that this war is truly the last great war. We are assured that this war will be the death of militarism, and then the lamb can safely cuddle up to the lion. Consequently, we have been told that, war on a large scale being now impossible, the United States needs no army and no navy, and that it would be folly to waste the taxpayers' money on such useless things.

Many believe that this country should set the other nations of the world a great moral example by pulling the teeth of our dogs of war, making them lambs, and inviting the lions to lie down with them, unheedful of the lesson of all ages that when the lion does lie down with the lamb, the lamb is always inside the lion.

Furthermore, we have been assured that the mere possession of armaments leads a nation to wage war, because being able to fight makes one want to fight; and that, obviously, the best way to avoid a fight is to be unable to fight.

I quote the following from Theodore Roosevelt's book, " America and the World War ":—

"These peace people have persistently and resolutely blinked facts. One of the peace congresses sat in New York at the very time that the feeling in California about the Japanese question gravely threatened the good relations between ourselves and the great empire of Japan. The only thing which at the moment could practically be done for the cause of peace was to secure some proper solution of the question at issue between ourselves and Japan. But this represented real effort, real thought. The peace congress paid not the slightest serious attention to the matter and instead devoted itself to listening to speeches which favored the abolition of the United States navy and even in one case the prohibiting the use of tin soldiers in nurseries because of the militaristic effect on the minds of the little boys and girls who played with them!"

When the prophet Isaiah told the Jews that there were big troubles brewing for them in the East, he spoke to unhearing ears, because unwilling ears. There were in those days, as in our day, the false prophets of peace who said that Isaiah was wrong; that there was no cause for worry about the indignation of Jehovah; that even at the worst His wrath could be appeased at any time, as necessity might arise, by a few burnt offerings and sacrificial mumblings. Their assurances were more pleasing than the warnings of Isaiah, so the Jews listened to the false prophets instead of to Isaiah, and they paid the penalty in Babylonian bondage.

The Isaiahs of true prophecy have long warned the people of this country that there is big trouble brewing for us in the East and in the Far East, and that we need armaments and men trained to arms to safeguard us against that trouble. These Isaiahs have told us that we cannot safeguard ourselves by any sacrifices made upon the altar of international brotherhood, or forefend ourselves against the great red peril of war by a few mumblings written down in arbitration treaties; but that we must have guns and men behind the guns. The Isaiahs who have been telling us these things are our true peace-advocates.

Those self-styled peace-men who are telling us that the best way to avoid war is to be unable to defend ourselves are not peace-men, but war-breeders. Though they emulate the dove in their cooing, they are far from being doves of peace. They ought to be styled dubs of peace. Their intentions may be good, yet they are enemies of peace, and betrayers of their country. Those who prevent the building of coast fortifications, which are our modern city gates, by advising against them, betray their country as actually as those who opened the gates of Rome to the hordes of Alaric.

Those who are trying to defeat our Congressional appropriations for a larger navy, for an adequate army, and for sufficient coast fortifications, although they may mean well, are as truly enemies of their country as if they should, in war, contribute to the armament and fighting force of an enemy, for the effect in both cases is identical.

Again I quote from Mr. Roosevelt:

"We object to the actions of those who do most talking about the necessity of peace because we think they are really a menace to the just and honorable peace which alone this country will in the long run support. We object to their actions because we believe they represent a course of conduct which may at any time produce a war in which we and not they would labor and suffer.

"In such a war the prime fact to be remembered is that the men really responsible for it would not

be those who would pay the penalty. The ultra-pacifists are rarely men who go to battle. Their fault or their folly would be expiated by the blood of countless thousands of plain and decent American citizens of the stamp of those, North and South alike, who in the Civil War laid down all they had, including life itself, in battling for the right as it was given to them to see the right."

But the false prophets of peace have assured us all along that there is no danger whatever of war between the United States and any other country. They tell us further that our armaments are a menace to other nations; that they evidence suspicion of other nations, and thereby place us under suspicion. According to such philosophy, the college man who becomes an athlete is a trouble-breeder, for the reason that the mere possession of muscle makes him a menace to other men.

Now, if we are in any danger of war, we ought to do the right thing to secure the safety of our country, of our homes and our families, and all things that are dear to us.

If it be true that the possession of armaments is an inducement for those who have them to use them, and if it be true that armaments fret the fighting spirit of other nations as a red rag frets a bull, and thereby lead to war, then, surely, we do not need more armaments, but less. Instead of arming ourselves any more, we should disarm until we are defenseless enough to be perfectly safe. On the other hand, if there be any likelihood that this country may be invaded by a foreign foe, we should be prepared to meet the invaders in the right way, and with the right spirit.

If it be the proper way to go and meet them as the inhabitants of Jerusalem went out to meet Alexander, with the keys to our gates, and with presents and sacrificial offerings, then we should adopt that way of preparing to pave their path with flowers and make them drunk on grape-juice and the milk of human kindness.

Dr. David Starr Jordan believes in disarmament. He further believes that armor-plate, guns, battleships, and ammunition should not be made by private manufacturers, but that, on the contrary, these things should be made exclusively by the government, for he is of the opinion that manufacturers of war materials foment disorder and promote war in order to bring themselves more business.

Long association with the manufacturers of war materials, especially of explosive materials, has enabled me to know whereof I speak, and I do know that such a belief is the utterest nonsense. The manufacturers of war materials with whom I am acquainted are among the staunchest of peace men, and they would no more be guilty of promot-

[7]

ing war to bring themselves business than a reputable surgeon would be likely to string a cord across the street to trip up pedestrians and break their limbs in order to bring himself business.

In the treatment of human physical ailments, we should deem it folly to confound remedy with disease, and to hold the physician responsible for pestilence. No one would think of looking upon our science of sanitation and our quarantine system as breeders and harbingers of pestilence, and no one would think that our laws against crime and our system of police protection tend to foster crime. Yet such is the attitude of many well-intentioned but overzealous persons with respect to our naval and military system and armaments. They consider them breeders and harbingers of war.

An army and navy are merely a mighty quarantine system against the pestilence of war. We must fortify our shores, police our seas with armor-clads, and be prepared to patrol the skies with aëroplanes around our entire national horizon when the need may come.

But it is urged that the people are overburdened with the cost of maintaining armies and navies. Assuming that the burden is great, was it ever less? Was it ever so small as it is now, compared with the numbers and wealth of the people? Again, cannot we well afford to bear a considerable burden of armaments as an insurance against war, and as a further insurance that if war comes, it will be far less deadly than it would be without them?

If Dr. Jordan were better acquainted with the manufacture of war materials, he would know that they can be made more cheaply, with equal excellence, by private concerns, than by the government. Furthermore, he would know that big manufacturers of war materials are obliged to employ a very large force of skilled labor, and that this labor has to be supplied employment when there are no government orders for war materials. For example, the manufacture of armorplate by the United States Steel Corporation is only a small part of that company's business. The manufacture of guns and armor-plate by the Bethlehem Steel Company does not keep it constantly occupied, and it has to furnish other employment for its men when government orders are not forthcoming. Consequently, it is obliged to make things besides armor-plate and guns and war materials.

The du Pont explosives companies do a far larger business in high explosives and smokeless powders for commercial purposes than they do for government purposes.

Therefore, if the manufacture of war materials were to be confined entirely to government shops, then the government would truly have to promote war to keep its employees busy. At any rate, the government would have to maintain a large labor force, making war materials alone, for the government could not devote itself to the manufacture of automobiles, chairs, cloth, artificial leather, dynamite, sporting powder, and the like, for commercial purposes, as private manufacturers do.

There is another reason why the private manufacturers of war materials should be encouraged by the government, and it is that, in the event of war, the government would find the large capital and plants of the wealthy Steel Trust, the Bethlehem Steel Company, and the du Ponts available for the purpose of national defense in addition to the government's own resources. This is very important.

The battle of Lake Erie was quite as much a du Pont victory as a Perry victory; for the resources, energy, and generalship of the du Pont Powder Company overcame inconceivable difficulties, carted the powder from Wilmington, Delaware, all the way overland to Lake Erie, and got it there on time.

It is unfortunate that a person's confidence in his knowledge of a subject is often directly proportionate to his ignorance of the subject. It is a psychological truth that ignorance may be taught, just like anything else, and a person may become very erudite in things which are not true, just as he may in things which are true.

Dr. Jordan, in recent public utterances, has said that he would rather the United States should lose its Pacific possessions than that we should go to war; and he has remarked that now, while the world is drunk with war, is a bad time to lay in more liquor. This is an ingenious metaphor, and well designed to trip the intelligence of the unwary. As a matter of fact, when the world is drunk with war, and rapine, murder, and plunder are rife, it is exactly the time to lay in more ammunition.

Had Dr. Jordan been in the position of Captain John Smith in the Virginia colony, when the Indians were on the war-path, he would have advised the settlers to disarm and destroy their stockades and forts. The Indians at that time went on the war-path and got drunk for war because they had a grievance.

When the present war is over and international commerce is re-established, we are destined to give some other nation a grievance, for the same reason that we then gave those Indians a grievance, and that other nation will go on the war-path, just as those Indians did, and that other nation when it takes up the torch and the sword and gets a taste of blood, is going to be as savage as the men engaged in the present European conflict.

There are two kinds of true prophets: The one kind, like Isaiah, who is directly inspired of God;

and the other kind, who judges the future by the lessons of the past. The scientist is a true prophet; but he is not one of the inspired kind. The way he does his predicting is the way of the astronomer, who uses a base line the width of the earth's orbit in order to triangulate the parallax of a star. So the scientific prophet triangulates the parallax of future events from a base line compassing all human history.

There is no one lesson which history teaches us more plainly than that the possession of wealth by a defenseless nation is a standing *casus belli* to other nations, and that always there has been the nation standing ready to attack and plunder any other nation when there was likely to be sufficient profit in the enterprise to pay for the trouble. Never have we seen any treaty stand for long in the way of such practices between nations. Treaties have always been mere scraps of paper, which, like the cobweb, ensnare the weak, while they let the strong break through.

It is strange that those who recommend that this country try the experiment of disarmament to secure peace by setting other nations a great moral example, should not have read history to see whether or not the experiment were a new one; and whether or not, judging by past experiments, it were likely to prove a success or a failure. Should these men look back through history, they would find that ancient Egypt tried the experiment, and went down under the sword and torch of fierce invaders from over the desert. They would learn that the Greeks tried the experiment and found it a failure. They would learn that India and China have bled through the ages because of their peaceableness. They would learn that the fall of Carthage was due not so much to the superior military power of Rome, or to the reiterations of Cato that Carthage must be destroyed, as it was to the peace talk of Hanno, which withheld the necessary support of Hannibal in Italy. They would learn that when old Rome lost her vigor and neglected her defenses, she was hewn to pieces by fierce barbarians. They would learn that the fathers of our own country, after the Revolution, tried the same old experiment, with the result that the city of Washington was captured and burned by the British in the war of 1812. They would learn, furthermore, that all prophets who have said that the nations will war no more, have been false prophets.

Four years before the Russo-Japanese war, I wrote an article for a New York magazine, in which I prophesied that war, and predicted Japanese victory. I predicted also at the same time that there would be in the near future a general European conflict. It has come.

The following quotations from that article may be of interest:

"*By far the greatest probability of imminent war lies in the Far East, between Russia and Japan. Japan feels the sting of the Russian whip that made her drop Port Arthur and withdraw from the continent of Asia, thus relinquishing the chief advantages gained by her victory over China. The whole sum paid Japan by China as a war indemnity has been expended on her navy and on armaments. In the East, in both naval and military strength, she is superior to Russia.*

"*Whether or not we shall soon have war will depend on whether Japan will quietly wait until Russia shall have finished the Trans-Siberian Railway, secured Korea, intrenched and fortified herself along the Asiatic coast, and built a fleet of sufficient strength entirely to overawe the little empire. It is doubtful if Japan will wait for the time when Russia shall be ready to strangle her. She may strike and drive Russia from Korea and secure, as well, a fair share of Chinese territory; or, what amounts to the same thing, a lease of a portion of the Celestial Empire. She will thereafter be better able to protect her interests in Chinese trade and opportunities. Should she strike soon, and she and Russia be left to themselves, Japan ought to win, for she is close at hand and will be able to bring to bear upon the points of collision a much greater force than Russia. She*

[14]

*will also be able to act with correspondingly
greater celerity.*

. . . .

*"If we would essay to predict future events,
we must draw the lines of divination in the direction that we see the nations grow, and these lines
must be parallel with those of great commercial
interests—be parallel with those of national self-
interests. We then have but one more question
to consider, on which to base à priori judgment.
It is the question of might—of national resources
and blood and iron.*

*"What was true on a small scale, with primi-
tive tribes of men, is also true on a large scale,
with the great world powers of today. In early
times, like the ebb and flow of the tides of the
sea, conquest and re-conquest, victory and defeat,
followed one another. Then destruction succeeded growth and growth destruction.*

*"As the great banyan tree constantly en-
croaches upon the territory of surrounding flora,
to overtop and blight and kill all upon which its
shadow falls, so do and so must nations in their
growth encroach upon their neighbors.*

*"In recent times, the tremendous strides made
in the arts and sciences, and the birth of new industries, and the enormous growth of all, have
provided room and occupation for the earth's
great dominating peoples. Vast land areas have*

been reclaimed, and boundless resources developed. Thus far the overflow has been upon the lands of the tameless American Indian—of the lazy African—of the docile Hindoo, and the simple savage of the southern seas. Now it is China's turn, and the wolves of greed, in the guise of trade, are already howling at her gates.

"Growth is proceeding with constantly accelerating rapidity, and soon the overflow must be on lands already filled to overflowing—not then with simple savages. It will then be Greek to Greek, over fortresses that frown along the whole frontier. Then there will be a clash. It is coming. Where the storm will first break, and when, is a question. That a great conflict will come, and at no distant date, is certain."—"The Home Magazine," July, 1900.

At the first annual banquet of the Aëronautical Society four years ago, I predicted exactly the use of the aëroplane in war that it has had since that time. President Taft was one of the speakers, and his subject was his pet peace and arbitration treaties. He said that there were not likely to be the requisite wars for testing out the aëroplane, as predicted. He said that there was going to be a shortage of wars.

Since that time, we have had the revolution in China, the Italian war with Tripoli, the Balkan wars, a continuous revolutionary performance in

Mexico, and finally, we have the present great European War. Not much of a shortage in wars, truly!

The following quotation from Dr. David Starr Jordan's " War and Waste " is an excellent illustration of the prophetic wisdom that is keeping the United States of America unprepared against war:

"What shall we say of the Great War of Europe, ever threatening, ever impending, and which never comes? We shall say that it will never come. Humanly speaking, it is impossible.

"Not in the physical sense, of course, for with weak, reckless, and godless men nothing evil is impossible. It may be, of course, that some half-crazed archduke or some harassed minister of state shall half-knowing give the signal for Europe's conflagration. In fact, the agreed signal has been given more than once within the last few months. The tinder is well dried and laid in such a way as to make the worst of this catastrophe. All Europe cherishes is ready for the burning. Yet Europe recoils and will recoil even in the dread stress of spoil-division of the Balkan war. . . .

"But accident aside, the Triple Entente lined up against the Triple Alliance, we shall expect no war. . . .

"The bankers will not find the money for such a

*fight, the industries of Europe will not maintain
it, the statesmen cannot. So whatever the bluster
or apparent provocation, it comes to the same
thing at the end. There will be no general war
until the masters direct the fighters to fight. The
masters have much to gain, but vastly more to
lose, and their signal will not be given."*

Eight years ago, when the great Peace Conference was held at Carnegie Hall, New York, to discuss the limitation and abolishment of armaments, the most notable of the pacifists represented were invited by the Economic Club of Boston to attend a banquet in that city for the free hot-airing of their views.

There was much sophistical palaver about destroying our old battle-flags and leveling our soldiers' monuments and all landmarks and reminders of war. William T. Stead, however, was more rational, and he was annoyed by the silly impracticable nonsense of some of the dubs of peace. Stead's better sense was evidenced by the fact that the following winter he recommended to the British Parliament that England build two battleships to every one built by Germany.

Invited to speak in defense of armaments, I held that we must arm for peace, and not disarm for it. I began my remarks by telling them this story:

In a small paragraph in an obscure place upon

the back page of a leading Boston paper, I once saw the announcement that Herbert Spencer, the great philosopher, was very ill, and not expected to live. On the front page of the same paper, under bold headlines, was a three-column article on the physical condition of John L. Sullivan.

John L. Sullivan was a fighter, while Herbert Spencer was only a philosopher; hence the difference in public interest.

John L. Sullivan, in his time, standing on the corner, would deplete the hall and break up any peace meeting in the world, and block the street with massed humanity for a square, jostling for a sight of him.

Several years ago, a reverend gentleman by the name of Charles Edward Jefferson elicited much applause by his public utterances on the blessings and advantages of non-resistance and meekness mild. He made it as clear as the day dawn of June, to the unreasoning, that it is all a mistake to build guns, warships, and coast fortifications; that our war colleges are not institutions of actual learning at all, but are institutions for teaching ignorance. He declared that militarism is squandering the taxpayers' money by the hundreds of millions, and all because the advocates of militarism and the friends of militarism are perverse and wilfully wot not what they do, though wisdom radiant as the rainbow stares them in the face; and because our military men, who have been educated at government expense and who, we have thought, were devoting their lives to the country's service in studying its needs and fighting its battles, are desirous merely of promotion and of widening the sphere of their activities.

According to Dr. Jefferson, these men are not what we have supposed them—a bulwark against trouble, but are trouble-makers, ignorant of the primary essential of their profession, namely militant meekness; and instead of being guardians of peace and an assurance against war, they are actual war-breeders. He seems to think that there is a real conspiracy to squander the taxpayers' money in the interest of a military clique.

A man may be wrong, and yet be honest. Prejudice is honest. Dr. Jefferson is doubtless honest, and if it should be that he is right, then his doctrine is practicable. If he is right, our military men are wrong. If our army and navy officers, who have been educated at the public expense and in the school of experience, do not know and understand better this country's needs in the respects and particulars for which they have been educated than does this good ecclesiastic, then it is proved that the church is a better military school than Annapolis or West Point. Theology, and not military science, should hereafter be taught in those institutions. The military parade should be called in from the campus and be replaced by knee drill in the chapel, and hereafter, at Annapolis, at West Point, and along the firing-line, the command should be Shoulder Psalms, instead of Shoulder Arms.

Let us lay down our arms and spike our guns, disband the military parade from the campus, as the sentimentalists desire us to do, and we shall very soon, with Kubla Khan, hear "ancestral voices [George Washington's among them] prophesying war."

CHAPTER II

CAN LAW BE SUBSTITUTED FOR WAR?

I AM a peace advocate—that is to say, I am one who advocates an active campaign in the cause of peace, employing the best means and instruments for the accomplishment of practical results.

Unfortunately, a wide difference of opinion exists in the ranks of those who style themselves peace advocates as to how the war against war can best be fought. That difference of opinion is as to whether we should arm for the fray, or disarm for it. Shall we go into the fight with sword and buckler, and with armor on, prepared to return blow with stronger blow; or shall we go into the fight with bared breasts, and, when we receive a blow upon one cheek turn the other cheek also, and let both our eyes be blackened and our nose be skinned in order to shame our antagonist, by giving him an object lesson of the horrors of war?

Ernst Haeckel has said there is nothing constant but change. He might have said also that there is a no more consistent thing in its constancy than human inconsistency.

That other great philosopher, Herbert Spencer, declared that, as he grew older, the more and more he realized the extent to which mankind is governed by irrationality.

Josh Billings said, "It is not so much the ignorance of men that makes them ridiculous as what they know that is not so."

The complex problems of ethics, eugenics, economics, and human dynamics, which enter into all questions and problems of peace and war, are like so many Chinese puzzles to the ordinary mind.

There are, broadly speaking, two kinds of minds —the ratiocinative and the irrational; in other words, the logical and the illogical. The logical mind proceeds scientifically from sure premises to just conclusions, taking no direction and traveling no faster and no farther in any direction than warranted and justified by ascertained fact. The irrational or illogical mind, on the contrary, is unable to discriminate between belief and knowledge, between facts and fancies. Consequently, this type of mind proceeds from guess to conclusion, with the result that final judgment is necessarily distorted, warped, and swerved from truth just in proportion as the basic guess is incorrect or false.

There is a no more momentous problem before the world today than that of international jurisprudence, especially with respect to the mainte-

nance of peace where practicable, and the control
of wars, when wars are inevitable or necessary;
and there is no subject of such moment more
fruitful of irrationalism.

In the light of practical common-sense, there
is nothing funnier in the writings of Mark Twain
than the inconsistent prating of our peace sophists. It is as though they let not their right-hand
brain know what their left-hand brain is doing.
They are usually brimmed and primed with sacrificial sentimentality and over-soul. Their deli-
catessen natures shrink from contact with the
stern, man-making realities of life. They are the
disciples of soft stuff. The mush and moonshine
of maudlin sentimentalism are their element.
They possess no powers of discrimination between
the actual and the erroneous. The guise of fact
is no recommendation to them unless it fits into
their scheme. An error is far more welcome if
it comes in a garmenture that conforms with their
ideals. They put their union label on what we receive by the grace of God, but they fail to recognize and appreciate that they cannot comprehend
the infinite; that what to them seems disorder
and confusion in the world may be the most perfect order in the eye of God. They cannot understand how infinite wisdom, infinite justice, and infinite mercy should have created a warring world;
consequently, they have set themselves the task
of repairing the faults of creation and of recreat-

ing the world to suit their own ideas as to what infinite wisdom and mercy ought to be.

When one of these peace sophists gets into a fight, however, he promptly prays to God to help him whip the other fellow. The pacific sentimentalist is usually a most arrant coward. In time of war, the cowardly sentimental pacifists are the loudest in appeals to Almighty God to fight on their side and to lead their army to victory—that same army which in time of peace they have done everything in their power to disarm and disband.

Recently, when speaking at a church, I was asked the question, "How long is it going to take to make might right?" I asked my interrogator this question: "If, at the creation, you had been consulted and your advice asked as to whether or not a world should be made in which all life should feed on other life, and half of the animal creation should be made prey for the other half; whether everything should be made tooth and nail, claw and scale, hunter and hunted, terror and blood, strife and war; whether or not the cat should train for the hunt by torturing the little bird— how would you have replied to God?" My querist did not answer me, but went home to think it over.

I do not purpose to make any apology for Infinite Wisdom. My pacifist friends are doing that constantly. It is my humble opinion that the

Creator did the best He could for us, and that we ought to be thankful and grateful.

I believe with Pope, that:

"Spite of pride, in erring reason's spite,
One truth is clear—whatever is, is right."

I realize that the most perfect order is confusion to the mind that is not constituted to comprehend it.

I know that the macrocosmic mechanism moves with mathematical exactitude, and that we, in comparison, are mighty only in our arrogance; that, in fact, we are but microscopic specks in the drift of worlds.

Nature seems to care little for individuals, but very much for races and species; little indeed for a person, very much for a people.

The terms, right and wrong, good and bad, are entirely relative. Right for an individual may not be so for a large aggregation of individuals. The welfare of a nation or a people may not be the welfare of the world, and God has His eye on the world.

The wrong are weak, the right are strong.
This mean the two terms right and wrong;
And truth sought out to any length,
Finds all wrong weakness, all right strength.

[26]

CAN LAW BE SUBSTITUTED FOR WAR?

FORMATIVE STRIFE

Primeval man found himself thrust into an environment where all animal life fed on other life, and half the animal creation was prey for the other half. He was one of the hunted. Yet, with less strength but greater cunning, he was destined to master all. Man's supremacy has been developed by warfare of wit, craft, and cunning, versus brute force.

Primitive man found himself "up a tree" in both the actual and the metaphoric sense. His teeth and claws were no match for those of the leopard and the sabre-toothed tiger. He had no recourse but flight until stern necessity taught him to wield a club.

Then he climbed down from his abode in trees, and began the conquest of the earth. The club made man a traveler. His forays with that weapon taught him to walk and fight upon his hind legs, and gave him his erect carriage. But he had to travel a long and thorny pathway indeed, armed only with a club, before he invented the stone hatchet and spear of sharpened flint or bone. It was a far-flung span across the gulf of time from the tree-home to the cave in the hill, his new abiding-place.

The bow and arrow, which enabled him to kill at long range, were his next weapon, and were the greatest invention of all time.

The protection of the heart with the left arm and shield, with the right arm free to wield the sword or hurl the javelin, made man right-handed.

Armed with the bow and arrow, spear and shield, man was equipped still better for travel; and ever since travel has been widening out the sky and broadening man's mental horizon.

The fighting spirit widened the acquaintance of different peoples, and the terrible menace of some savage common enemy forced different tribes to unite and build up nations. Union against danger is the best instructor of self-government, and the best guarantee of internal good behavior.

It is generally recognized that man is a product of his environment; that he is in body and mind the sum of his own and ancestral experiences; that he is omnivorous; that he drinks water and breathes air; and yet, many persons fail to recognize the inevitable concomitant conclusion that he is also of necessity a warring animal, and that the formative influences of the fierce struggle for existence have made him what he is. His life is a series of reactions to environing stimuli; and he is actuated and shaped by those stimuli, and just as those stimuli have been necessary to his growth, so they are still necessary to his continued growth, and even to his very existence. In other words, the formative influences that have made and sustained man are still necessary to his maintenance.

The character of the strife may be changed, and is already largely changed, from war to business. But the intensity of the struggle cannot be alleviated one whit, because it is impossible, in the nature of things, to maintain man's strength of character in any other way. He could live a little longer without strife than without food or air or water, but the absence of strife would be as fatal to him in the end as would be the absence of food, air, or water.

The struggle for existence has always been a business proposition with man, and business today is a struggle for existence as intense and merciless as the struggle in war.

In olden times, piracy and war for plunder were the principal business of mankind. Today, business is a warfare, and though it may be law-abiding, still the weak go down under it and suffer and die under it as surely as they did in old-time wars. The relation of strength to weakness remains unchanged, and the reward for strength and the penalty for weakness are as great as they ever were.

There now exists, as always, the same intensity of incentive of all classes to strive for something more and something better than they have. Though the condition of all classes has improved, the struggle of individual with individual is as great, the strife of class with class is as intense as ever.

The ownership of one's earnings, with freedom to apply and enjoy them, was the greatest prize ever offered to stimulate the working genius of this world, and the results during the past hundred and fifty years have been phenomenal.

The world has progressed more within that time in those things which tend to complete living than it had previously progressed in all the ages that had dragged their slow length along since the world thawed out of the ancient ice.

But human agencies, like all agencies in nature, are essentially rhythmical. In order to accumulate the necessary energy and enthusiasm to go far enough in the right direction, we inevitably go too far, and, when the pendulum returns, it swings to the other extreme.

It is important to realize the great truth that freedom ends when it aims beyond the spirit which strives for the greatest good to the greatest number.

According to Herbert Spencer, the criminal classes are composed of those who have been pushed out of the race in the struggle for existence under modern conditions. They were normal components of society in the past, when all men were soldiers and all soldiers were bandits, and the principal business of mankind was piracy and war for plunder.

There being no longer the ever-present opportunity to join in an inter-tribal or an international war for robbery, the soldier-bandit now makes war upon society.

All of the Huns and Vandals in our midst are today armed with the short-sword of the ballot. How important it is then that they should be taught to know and to understand that in the use of this weapon their work should be formative and not deformative; that it should be constructive and not destructive!

SUBSTITUTION OF LAW FOR WAR

The poet's words, "The parliament of man, the federation of the world," have become a very familiar quotation in recent years. Anciently all wisdom was taught in poesy, and we have never yet quite freed ourselves from the age-long habitude of receiving as unimpeachable wisdom whatever may be said in verse.

To the common mind, a statement in didactic verse has the proselyting power of Holy Writ. Now, this line of Tennyson, "The parliament of man, the federation of the world," points us toward a Utopia, without hope of actual attainment.

There is at the present time a growing good intention to put an end to wars by international conciliation and arbitration; in short, to substitute law for war. We must, however, keep strongly in mind the interdependence of law and force, and the consequent interdependence of international law and armaments. Conciliation must not be confounded with arbitration, and persuasion must not be confounded with law.

Law has been aptly designated "codified custom." Actually, law is an attempt to construct experience into prophecy. We are able to judge of the sufficiency of new laws only by the sufficiency of laws in past practice.

The error is very common, to confound as having the same meaning terms of quite opposite meanings—for example, it is a very common error to confound society with government, and civilization with enlightenment. Society is an order of things by virtue of which we are able to co-operate with one another and to enjoy mutuality of possessions which gives them their only value; while government is an order of things for the purpose of protecting society.

The world has arrived at great enlightenment, and has attained some degree of civilization. Self-interest is becoming more and more altruistic, and altruism is becoming more and more profitable. We are not so barbarous as we used to be, but we still slaughter one another to adjust international differences. This cannot be esteemed civil procedure. Enlightenment may be very uncivil, and civility may not be enlightenment.

The great problem yet remains of uniting under

practical laws the nations of the earth into a family of nations.

This is not a work for dreamers or sentimentalists; but is purely a business proposition, which can be effected only to the extent that the best interests of all the contracting parties are thereby secured.

When will arbitration be able to realize the Utopian dreams of the pacifists? General Homer Lea answers the question once for all in the following expressive terms:

"Only when arbitration is able to unravel the tangled skein of crime and hypocrisy among individuals can it be extended to communities and nations. Thence will International Arbitration come of its own accord as the natural outgrowth of national evolution through the individual. As nations are only man in the aggregate, they are the aggregate of his crimes and deception and depravity, and so long as these constitute the basis of individual impulse, so long will they control the acts of nations.

"When, therefore, the merchant arbitrates with the customer he is about to cheat; when trusts arbitrate with the people they are about to fleece; when the bulls and bears arbitrate with the lambs they are about to shear; when the thief arbitrates with the man he is about to rob, or the murderer with his victim, and so on throughout the category

of crime, then will communities be able to dispense with laws, and international thievery and deception, shearing and murder, resort to arbitration."

The men who control our city and state politics and make and enforce our city and state laws all over the country are not always honest, but, on the contrary, they are often notoriously corrupt, notwithstanding the fact that they have much stronger incentives to be honest here than they would have in dealing with foreign nations and strange peoples. What, therefore, are we to expect of their integrity and their honesty in the settlement of international disputes and in the enactment and execution of international laws?

What an enormous field for graft it will be when some weaker nation tries to get its rights at the coming international tribunal!

Our laws are now notoriously inadequate with respect to theft, burglary, highway robbery, and municipal-government graft. The amount of money loss to the people of this country through the failure of our laws to suppress these iniquities is enough to support a standing army of half a million men, build four battleships a year, and place us on such a defensive footing as absolutely to preclude all danger of war with any foreign power.

Has human nature improved so much lately that

special privilege will no longer result from special power? Has the human race progressed so much lately that privilege and oppression will not follow power; wealth and luxury follow privilege; and degeneracy and disorganization follow wealth and luxury?

The race has certainly not so altered that men do not grow old and die; and nations, like men, have their youth, their middle age, their decrepitude and death.

Periodically, some religio-pathological sect will announce the conclusion of an understanding with the Great Reaper, whereby, through certain incantations or breathing exercises, death may be indefinitely postponed; but they, like other mortals, keep on dying.

Those good men who are the leaders in the present peace movement must realize the fact that the carrying out of their project will devolve, not upon them—not upon the philanthropist, the sentimentalist, and the humanitarian—but upon the politician.

The actual procedure of the Hague congresses enables us to forecast exactly this result. The judicial bench of that court was a bargain-counter, over which political advantage was bartered for political advantage. It was no real love of peace that dominated those tribunals: only the powerful nations spoke or were heard. No protection was suggested for the weaker nations, who, presumably, would be most benefited by international arbitration. They were quite out of the running.

International arbitration will ultimately become a political machine. Nothing can prevent it, and there is no reason to believe that those politicians who will have control of the international arbitration machine will be any more honest than other machine politicians.

ALL LAW MUST BE BACKED BY FORCE

It is a popular belief that when the paradoxical conciliatory legal persuasion in the form of arbitration goes into effect, we shall no longer require any armaments, but may forge our swords into plow-shares and spears into pruning-hooks, disband our armies, and return the soldiers to the shops and farms.

We are prone to forget that law is as much a representative of the requisite power behind it for its enforcement as a paper dollar is a representative of the requisite gold available for its redemption. A well-known orator came very near becoming President through a popular misconception as to the interdependence of gold and paper money, and he failed to get the Presidency because of a public awakening to the error.

We are prone to forget, furthermore, that it is the respect for power behind law that makes possible its enforcement. Any law to adjust international differences by arbitration will simply be an embodiment of the collective wisdom of allied Powers in the exercise of force, and a force that is representative of their banded armies and navies.

International law is static military force. War is the dynamic form of the same force. I believe in international arbitration for all it is worth. It is a good thing to push along. It will unquestionably lessen the frequency of wars, but many wars are sure to come in spite of it, and because of it.

Non-Justiciable Differences

There are ills of national bodies politic that can be cured only by the sword. Insurmountable differences between various nations and races of men are always sure to arise, as impossible to arbitrate as the differences between the herbivora and the carnivora.

The existence of the carnivora depends upon the sacrifice of the herbivora. Their interests are, from their very nature, antagonistic, and their differences are, by consequence, insurmountable, and not justiciable. The harmony of nature depends upon inharmony between the meat-eaters and the vegetable-eaters, and the harmony of modern progress has likewise depended in large measure upon formative inharmony between peoples.

Such radical differences and such concomitant radical diversity of interests exist among the various races of men that the task of harmonizing their interests, aims, and activities will be about as great as would be that of bleaching their skins to a uniform color.

It is a practical impossibility to enact international laws that will make the welfare of each nation the concern of all, with no subordination of any one to the welfare of another. Will arbitration be able to place all peoples upon a plane of equality? Will it be able to secure to all, even the meanest, equal rights to enjoyment of property, life, liberty, and the pursuit of happiness?

Will arbitration be able to make the Anglo-Saxon, the Teuton, the African, and the Oriental meet one another on common ground, and share and share alike, live and let live, when their interests come into collision?

If arbitration cannot do this—if arbitration does not do this—if it does not treat all with strict impartiality, then those who are ill-treated are going to rebel, and wars will still come.

Between nations no sentimental consideration exists or is possible, sufficiently effectual to exert more than the merest microscopic influence as a deterrent of war. Self-interest always has been, and always will be, the deciding factor in the settlement of international disputes. War uncloaks international hypocrisy, and the people are seen in their true character.

The attitude of the warlike and powerful nations in the past toward the weaker nations has been very similar to that of the carnivora toward the herbivora.

International arbitration may somewhat lessen the burden of armaments, but the time will be long before it can lift the burden. The orators who plead at the International Tribunal will speak in the voice of the deep-throated guns behind them; their persuasion will be that of cold steel, and neither brotherly love nor international sympathy will be their guide, but self-interest, and no demands will be relinquished except from policy in their observance of such rights of others as are warded by the frowning ramparts of opposing force.

Unless all the nations of the world join in the pact, then arbitration will simply be an alliance for the benefit of the allies themselves as against all others. There will be nothing new in such an arrangement. The Six Nations of New York did the same thing; they formed a federation and settled their differences by arbitration, and it was a good thing for the Six Nations; but it was not a good thing for the neighboring Indian tribes.

We Americans expect to get all we want any way, either with or without arbitration. If we expected that the Chinese would be forced upon

us, or our rights and privileges curtailed in the
Orient, we should not think of joining in an arbitration pact for a minute.

There will always be the warfare of commerce
for the markets of the world, and it will be tempered with avarice, not mercy; and commercial
warfare will become more and more severe as the
nations grow, and as competition, with want and
hunger behind it, gets keen as the sword-edge
with the crowding of people into the narrow world.

Unchanging Human Nature

Human nature is the same today as it was in
the ante-rebellion days of human slavery. It is
the same as it was when Napoleon, with the will-
o'-the-wisp of personal and national glory held
before the eyes of emotional and impressionable
Frenchmen, led them to wreck for him the monarchies of Europe. Human nature is the same today as it was in Cæsar's time, when he massacred
two hundred and fifty thousand Germans—men,
women, and children—in a day, in cold blood,
while negotiations for peace were pending, and entered in his diary the simple statement, "Cæsar's
legions killed them all." Human nature is the
same today as it was in the cruel old times, when
war was the chief business of mankind, and popu-
lations sold as slaves were among the most profitable plunder. Yes, human nature is the same

as it has always been. Education and Christian teaching have made pity and sympathy more familiar to the human heart, but avarice and the old fighting spirit are kept in leash only by the dominance of necessity and circumstances, which the institutions of civilization impose upon the individual.

The following is quoted from "Origins and Destiny of Imperial Britain," by the late Professor J. A. Cramb:

"War may change its shape, the struggle here intensifying it, there abating it; it may be uplifted by ever loftier purposes and nobler causes. But cease? How shall it cease?

"Indeed, in the light of history, universal peace appears less as a dream than as a nightmare, which shall be realized only when the ice has crept to the heart of the sun, and the stars, left black and trackless, start from their orbits."

Max Müller has told us that the roots of some of our words are older than the Egyptian Pyramids. Far older still are the essential traits of human nature. The human nature of today will be the human nature of tomorrow, and the human nature of tomorrow will be in all essential respects the same as it was in ancient Rome, Persia, and Egypt, and even in the palmy days of sea-sunk Atlantis.

The best of us are at heart barbarians under a thin veneer of civilization, and it is as natural for us to revert to barbarous war as for the hog to return to his wallow.

If we were able to apply to the upbuilding of our Army and Navy the money that goes to political graft throughout the country, and the money that has been squandered, and is still being squandered through our notorious vote-purchasing pensions, we could place ourselves upon a war footing that would be an absolute guarantee of permanent peace. It is not, therefore, very encouraging, to enlarge this failing system of laws, in order to save an annual expenditure certainly less than what the defects of our laws now cost the country.

Even though international wars may be prevented by a court of arbitration, can rebellion and civil war be prevented, and ought they always to be prevented?

JUSTIFIABLE WARS

When the unjust laws of an iniquitous government make existence intolerable for the great mass of the people of a country or of a colonial possession; "when in the course of human events, it becomes necessary" for a people to throw off the yoke of oppression, as we did in our War of the Revolution, or as the French people did in the French Revolution, or as the great Chinese people have lately done by their rebellion against the domination of an intolerable savage Manchu monarchy, then war is the only remedy, and freedom can then plead only with the sword.

I quote the following from Theodore Roosevelt's "America and the World War":

"In 1864 there were in the North some hundreds of thousands of men who praised peace as the supreme end, as a good more important than all other goods, and who denounced war as the worst of all evils. These men one and all assailed and denounced Abraham Lincoln, and all voted against him for President. Moreover, at that time there were many individuals in England and France who said it was the duty of those two nations to mediate between the North and the South, so as to stop the terrible loss of life and destruction of property which attended our Civil War; and they asserted that any Americans who in such event refused to accept their mediation and to stop the war would thereby show themselves the enemies of peace. Nevertheless, Abraham Lincoln and the men back of him by their attitude prevented all such effort at mediation, declaring that they would regard it as an unfriendly act to the United States. Looking back from a distance of fifty years, we can now see clearly that Abraham Lincoln and his supporters were right. Such mediation would have been a

[43]

hostile act, not only to the United States but to humanity. The men who clamored for unrighteous peace fifty years ago this fall were the enemies of mankind."

Those who are oppressed by the superincumbent weight of society, and labor for mere existence, with no hope of freedom from poverty, are slaves as much as were those made bondsmen in old-time wars. It matters little whether the wolf at the door be a creature of sociological conditions, or a creature of war. The evil is no less real.

James Russell Lowell, in his admirable poem on France and the French Revolution, said about the most expressive, the most potential, and altogether the best thing that has ever been said illustrative of the uncontrollable massiveness of the popular will, which, under the stimulus of patriotism or the smart or burden of accumulated wrongs, can stampede a nation into war:

"As, flake by flake, the beetling avalanches
  Build up their imminent crags of noiseless snow,
Till some chance thrill the loosened ruin launches
  And the blind havoc leaps unwarned below,
So grew and gathered through the silent years
  The madness of a People, wrong by wrong.
There seemed no strength in the dumb toiler's
      tears,

CAN LAW BE SUBSTITUTED FOR WAR?

*No strength in suffering;—but the Past was
    strong:*
The brute despair of trampled centuries
*   Leapt up with one hoarse yell and snapt its
        bands,*
*   Groped for its rights with horny, callous hands,*
And stared around for God with bloodshot eyes."

The justification of war depends entirely upon
the conditions which produce it. In short, war is
justifiable only when it is a remedy for evils
greater than the evils of the war. War is sometimes a very bitter remedy; nevertheless, there
are diseases much worse than the remedy. The
horrors of the French Revolution, bad as they
were, remedied a condition still more horrible, for
the condition of the French common people,
"bowed by the weight of centuries," had become
so abject that life was intolerable; no change
could be for the worse. Under such circumstances
there is no fear of death; the fear of death is only
fear of the loss of life through love of life. When
existence is intolerable, and there is no hope in
the heart for better things, life, having no value,
is not much loved, and death has no terrors.

In spite of all the bloodshed of the reign of
terror, in spite of all who fell under the leader-
ship of Napoleon, the French people were benefited by the Revolution a thousand-fold more than
they were injured by it.

If arbitration could prevent such wars, which are man's God-given privilege that a people may secure its inalienable rights, then arbitration, in that respect, would be an iniquitous thing.

War, at best, is a horrible business. It is a reversion to the brute force of primitive savagery, and is never justifiable except in the extremity of last resort. But we must appreciate and acknowledge the fact that the horrors of war, the sacrifice of treasure, the sacrifice of life, are no arguments whatever against war when inalienable human rights are at stake that must be fought for, and that are worth the sacrifice.

There are at times objects and obligations which are worth the sacrifice. To prevent war in such cases would be a disgrace and a crime.

As Admiral Mahan says, "Even the material evils of war are less than the moral evil of compliance with wrong."

CHRISTIANITY AND WAR

In 1901, the editor of *The Christian Herald* requested me to write an article in answer to the following question: "Is it consistent for a loyal Christian, who believes that war is contrary to the teachings of the Prince of Peace, to engage in the manufacture of material designed exclusively for the purpose of war?"

In my reply, I pointed out that the great majority of Christians throughout the world, while they hate war, are often called upon themselves to become warriors and to fight for their doctrine of peace. The Rev. T. De Witt Talmage was chosen to reply to my article, which he did by agreeing with all I had said.

According to the annals of history, wars have almost invariably been caused by one party attempting to rob another party, or one people another people. On such occasions, it is self-evident that the blame for the wars rested with the robbers. Those who fought in defense of their lives and property, although actual participants in warfare, were guiltless.

Of course, the attempt to rob and plunder has sometimes been mutual, and both participants have been aggressors, as were Napoleon and Alexander in the Russian war. In the great majority of cases, however, one side has been on the aggressive, and the other on the defensive.

When an officer of the law catches an evil-doer in the act, and is attacked by him, if, in making an arrest, the officer is compelled to draw his own revolver and shoot the malefactor, he does a justifiable act. We have here war in miniature, and it may be taken as a type of all wars. While we are free to grant that wars are wrong, yet the wrong rests entirely with the offenders, instead of with the defenders, of human right.

Housebreaking is wrong, yet the brave knight

who, in mediæval times, breached a castle wall to free some prisoner unjustly held, did a wholly commendable act. Similarly, one nation which raises an army to free from bondage slaves held by another nation, does an equally commendable act, and the blame for the war rests with those who hold the slaves.

War is an ugly and an awful thing, while some peace theories are very beautiful, and they are quite safe in times of peace; but when, in the past, slaves had to be freed, then the true Christians took down their old swords and shouldered their old guns, and went to the front. If we read the inscriptions on the monuments erected to the memory of those who died in our great Civil War, we find it was an army of Christians who fell.

War is often a necessity. It cannot always be avoided, and, when it comes, we want the best tools we can get with which to fight. It is criminal negligence for a nation not to be prepared against war. It is criminal negligence for a great nation not to be abreast of the times in arms and equipment.

Often at the bayonet's point, trade and civilization and even Christianity, have been forced upon the savage, and upon exclusive and unwarlike peoples, and now Christianity, civilization, and militarism, sisters of strange relation, hand in hand, embrace the world.

In "Sartor Resartus" Carlyle says:

CAN LAW BE SUBSTITUTED FOR WAR?

"The first ground handful of nitre, sulphur, and charcoal drove Monk Schwartz's pestle through the ceiling. What will the last do?"

His own answer is that it will

". . . achieve the final undisputed prostration of force under thought, of animal courage under spiritual."

Again Carlyle says, in the same work:

"Such I hold to be the genuine use of gunpowder: that it makes all men alike tall. Nay, if thou be cooler, cleverer than I, if thou have more mind, though all but no body whatever, then canst thou kill me first, and art the taller. Hereby, at last is the Goliath powerless and the David resistless; savage animalism is nothing, inventive spiritualism is all."

What does the Bible say about Christ's mission of peace?

"And suddenly there was with the angel a multitude of the heavenly host praising God and saying, Glory to God in the highest, and on earth peace, good will toward men" (Luke II : 13, 14).

[49]

"And thou, child, shalt be called the Prophet of the Highest . . . to guide our feet into the way of peace" (Luke I : 76, 79).

"And his name shall be called . . . The Prince of Peace" (Is. IX : 6).

I hold that there is nothing whatever in the foregoing quotations inconsistent with warring for the right. From the nature of things, war is often the price of peace, and justice can only be enforced by the sword. In the great American Rebellion it was the voice of guns alone that could command the emancipation of the slaves.

An apostle of the Prince of Peace may often best serve his Master by becoming a good soldier. The Christian armies that turned back and drove out of Europe the invading Moors rendered their Master better service than had they, in order to escape war, fled before the advancing hosts of Islam.

Should China and India become really aroused and advance during the next twenty-five years as rapidly as has Japan during a like period in the past, and should the great "Yellow Peril" rise in its might, and threaten the Christian World, is there a single soldier of the Cross now enlisted in the cause of Peace who would not then buckle on his cartridge-belt, shoulder his gun, and go and fight in the defense of his religion and his home?

I must confess my belief that, if invasion were threatened on the Atlantic Coast, some of the pacifists I have met would not buckle on the cartridge-belt, but would, on the contrary, gird up their loins, take the advice of Horace Greeley, and go West.

Let us again quote from the Scriptures:

"The Lord is a man of war" (Ex. XV : 3).

"The Lord of Hosts is his name" (Is. LI : 15).

"Blessed be the Lord my strength, which teacheth my hands to war, and my fingers to fight" (Ps. CXLIV : 1).

It is evident that the modern Christian misunderstands Christ's true mission, for he said:

"Think not that I am come to send peace on earth: I came not to send peace, but a sword" (Matt. X : 34).

"I am come to send fire on the earth" (Luke XII : 49).

"And he that hath no sword, let him sell his garment and buy one. . . . for the things concerning me have an end" (Luke XXII : 36, 37).

[51]

St. Paul said:

"For he is the minister of God to thee for good. But if thou do that which is evil, be afraid; for he beareth not the sword in vain; for he is the minister of God, a revenger to execute wrath upon him that doeth evil" (Rom. XIII : 4).

Dr. Lyman Abbott, who is one of the best of America's big men, and one of the biggest of America's best men, has the following to say about war:

"I am not, therefore, one of those who think that war is always wrong. I cannot think that Jesus Christ Himself inculcated the doctrine that force never could be used—He who, when He saw the traders in the Temple, did not wait to argue with them nor to appeal to their conscience, for He knew that they had neither reason nor conscience, but drove them out with a whip of small cords, driving the cattle before Him and overturning the tables of the money-changers and letting the money roll upon the floor. I am not afraid to follow Him with whatsoever force it may be necessary for righteousness to put on, when unrighteousness has armed herself to commit wrong. I cannot think all war is wrong. If I did, I should not want to look upon a Bunker Hill Monument, for it would be a monument to our

shame; I should want never to speak the name of Gettysburg, for my lips would blister and my cheeks would blush; I should want to bury in the grave of oblivion the names of Washington and Grant."

There can be but one interpretation of Christian duty and but one interpretation of true peace. Without justice, the mere absence of war does not constitute peace to the Christian. Neither to the Christian is warfare waged in the interest of justice incompatible with the peace principles which underlie his religious faith. Therefore, the true interpretation of peace is absence of war, where justice reigns, and the true Christian mission is to see that justice be done, for without it there can be no righteous peace. Such peace as can reign with injustice becomes the abettor of injustice.

While I believe in international conciliation and arbitration, peace and good will, I do not believe in unlimited arbitration. I do not believe that arbitration can ever be a universal panacea with which all evils can be cured without resort to firearms. There are times when throats have to be cut, and when God is on the side of the executioner.

When a nation persists perennially in war, it can only be brought to peace by some other nation which will meet it on the battlefield. Christ established the dictum that they who take the sword shall perish by the sword. War begets war. The sword brings the sword. As Napoleon said about sparing murderers and abolishing capital punishment, *"Que messieurs les assassins commencent."*

We want to put a stop to wars to save life. I wonder why it is that we are not equally anxious to prevent loss of life from other causes besides war. Why are we not equally interested in preventing the tremendous loss of life from easily preventable railroad disasters? An international movement for safety equipment and sanitation, with an enlistment of effort and money equal to that being devoted to this great peace movement would save many more lives every year than the annual loss in the Napoleonic wars.

Dr. Strong, President of the American Institute of Social Service, stated at a dinner several years ago, that the number of persons killed and wounded every year in the United States alone by railroad accidents, steamship accidents, workshop accidents, accidents in the streets, and other accidents—all very largely due to preventable causes—amounts to more than 500,000. In the Japanese-Russian war a total of 333,786 men were killed and wounded on both sides, not counting the losses in naval battles. During the same period in the United States alone the great army of American laborers engaged in manufacturing and building operations suffered a loss of 425,000 killed and injured; 92,000 more were therefore killed and injured in our industries in one year than during that entire war.

I wonder why it is that we are not as enthusiastic in this social-service work as we are in attacking the problem of war. Is it that there is more glory and more that appeals to the martial imagination in attacking war and warriors than there is in the prosaic, tame, and glamourless enterprise of simply saving human life in peaceful pursuits for the mere sake of saving it? Is it the old war spirit in the breasts of the peace men that moves them? Are they fighters, too? In attacking war, do they feel that they are somehow identified with the pomp and circumstance of glorious war?

CHAPTER III

OUR INCONSISTENT MONROE DOCTRINE

" If you want war, nourish a doctrine. Doctrines are the most frightful tyrants to which men ever are subject, because doctrines get inside of a man's own reason and betray him against himself."
William Graham Sumner, " War and Other Essays."

A DOCTRINE is a creed, usually mandatory, framed by one person or set of persons, for the belief or conduct of another person or set of persons. A doctrine is not necessarily based upon principles of right, equity, justice, or even expediency.

Doctrines are directions written on the guide-boards of fanaticism. An exact truth is never proclaimed as a doctrine: there is no doctrine of mathematics.

The Monroe Doctrine, which pledged the United States to defend American republican institutions, north and south, against monarchical encroachments from the Old World, with the dependable support of England, was proclaimed in 1823, mainly in response to a Continental doctrine called the Holy Alliance, formed in 1815 by and between Austria, Russia, Prussia, and France. The Holy Alliance was in effect a system of mutual political monarchical insurance, under which the forces of the allied Powers could be used to subdue revolution against the institution of kingship.

The French Revolution, followed by the democratic empire of Napoleon, had severely shaken the old intolerant and intolerable order of things. The Holy Alliance was an expedient of the old order to insure itself against democratic institutions.

A revolution in Spain in 1820 was promptly suppressed by the Holy Alliance, and the Spanish people, who had raised their heads and begun to look around for freedom, were again bowed under the yoke of the detested Bourbons. The Holy Alliance was surely a most unholy alliance.

Russia, by a ukase in 1821, claimed the right to keep the vessels of all other Powers out of the North Pacific Ocean. That was a Russian "Monroe Doctrine" which helped to make Monroe a doctrinaire.

In 1823 Spain lost, through revolutions, all of her American possessions except Cuba and Porto Rico, and Portugal had lost Brazil. France had lost the island of Haiti.

The United States naturally sympathized with the newly-formed states built on the ruins of the Spanish and Portuguese empires. They had mostly adopted republican institutions, becoming sisters of the great northern republic.

James Monroe was not the father of the child named for him, for the actual formulator of the Monroe Doctrine was John Quincy Adams, at that time Secretary of State, who got the cue from George Canning.

England wanted unrestricted trade with the Spanish-American countries; she had no need of additional territory on the American continent, but she saw danger in its acquisition by other nations. George Canning tried four times in 1823 to get the United States to join England in her declaration of the open-door policy. Monroe favored the proposal, but finally Adams convinced the President that it would be better to avoid any entangling arrangement with England, and to stand alone.

On the second of December, 1823, in his annual message to Congress, President Monroe made the following declaration on behalf of the United States:

"The American continents, by the free and independent condition which they have assumed and maintain, are henceforth not to be considered as subjects for future colonization by European powers. . . . We should consider any attempt on their part to extend their system to any portion of this hemisphere as dangerous to our peace and safety. With the existing colonies or dependencies of any European power we have not

interfered and shall not interfere. But with the governments who have declared their independence and maintained it, and whose independence we have, on great consideration and on just principles, acknowledged, we could not view any interposition for the purpose of oppressing them or controlling, in any other manner, their destiny, by any European power, in any other light than as the manifestation of an unfriendly disposition toward the United States."

Such was the birth of the famous Monroe Doctrine. Its recognition by England made it effective. The Monroe Doctrine has nothing whatever to do with international law. It is simply an expression of British national policy for the United States.

Our diplomacy, being a branch of our politics, is often inconsistent with our national policy. American justification for the doctrine appears to have been mainly dependent upon the fact that we had no intentions of encroaching upon the spheres of influence of any of the nations of the Old World, but that we intended to safeguard what we conceived to be our legitimate sphere of influence.

The American Republic was very young when the Monroe Doctrine was proclaimed—a doctrine which, as one writer has said, is "the most magnificent bluff in all history, and so far the most successful.''

During the American Civil War, France, with the connivance of England, conceived the plan of establishing in Mexico the empire of Maximilian. We were too busy at the time, settling some little differences of opinion within our family of states, to exact recognition of our protest. After the memorable exchange of compliments and courtesies between Grant and Lee at Appomattox, however, Uncle Sam indicated to Napoleon the Little that the Imperialists must be kicked out. Lacking the support of France, they were kicked out by the Mexicans.

While through the Monroe Doctrine the United States served notice on the nations of the Old World to keep hands off the American continent, the doctrine at the same time constituted an implied promise on our part to keep hands off any territory beyond the confines of America. So long as the policies of Great Britain did not run counter to our Monroe Doctrine, it was destined to be quite effective in preventing land-grabbing on the American continent by other European Powers. But the Monroe Doctrine possesses an innate dog-in-the-manger aspect, certain some day to bring trouble, for the great nations of the world have far outgrown the expectations of our forefathers; their commerce has become an inseparable part of the commerce of South American

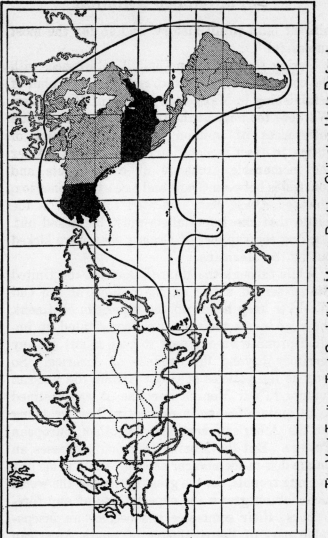

The Vast Territory That Our Inflated Monroe Doctrine Obligates Us to Defend

countries, and their interests in like measure have become identified with the interests of those countries. Just to the extent that their welfare and the welfare of the South American republics become mutual are they likely to be brought into collision with the Monroe Doctrine, and, when the collision comes, it means war, unless the United States abandons that doctrine.

Our self-assumed protectorate over the South American republics is not welcomed by those countries. They resent our arrogance. We have never cultivated trade with them, nor joined them in the development of their industries, and have never financed their enterprises. Even when an American citizen has paid a visit to a South American country, he has first found it necessary to go to England and take ship from there.

The European countries, on the other hand, have promoted business relations with the South American republics, have supplied them with working capital and cultivated their friendship, confidence, and respect, while we have done nothing of the sort.

The citizens of the United States whom the South Americans have seen in their dominions have usually been adventurous, irresponsible fortune-hunters. Their trouble-breeding propensities have not tended to foster amicable feeling between the great Republic of the North and her Southern sisters.

So long as the Monroe Doctrine did not circumscribe the ambitions of the United States the institution possessed some semblance of vitality; but, when the explosion came that blew up the *Maine,* it also exploded the Monroe Doctrine, for immediately the United States, abandoning its time-honored policy of keeping within American confines, and out of entangling alliances and complications with other nations, reached out a grasping hand and seized upon the Far Pacific possessions of Spain, right at the door of China and within the legitimate sphere of influence of Japan. Yet, curiously enough, we still adhere to the old proclamation, America for the Americans, oblivious of the equal right of China and Japan to proclaim, Asia for the Asiatics.

Several years ago, I spoke at a luncheon of the Twentieth Century Club in Boston. I was seated beside a noted Japanese diplomat. He said, "Mr. Maxim, you have a Monroe Doctrine —America for the Americans; we also have a similar doctrine—Asia for the Asiatics; but we are not ready to enforce ours yet, and you are not ready, and are not likely to be ready, to enforce yours. A little later, we shall inquire by what logic you can proclaim America for the Americans, and disclaim our right equally to proclaim Asia for the Asiatics."

The Japanese are a far-seeing and a patient people. They know how to wait, but they know also when to strike, and how to strike with the force of a Jovian thunderbolt. They are no longer merely a cute little picture-book people. They have risen with stupendous strides into a very eminent position as a World-Power, a Power to be reckoned with. They are different from us, but we have no right to consider them our inferiors. They may very possibly prove to be our superiors. A government of the people and for the people is a failure if the government does not take measures for the adequate defense of the people. Self-preservation is the first law of nature. Consequently, it is a law which must be observed as the chief element of greatness.

I quote the following from "The Valor of Ignorance," by General Homer Lea:

"How unreasonable is it to expect that the combined nations of Europe, with all their military strength, shall remain restricted to one-twelfth of this world's land, burrowed into and hewn over for the last thousand years, while this Republic, without armies, shall maintain dominion over one-half the unexploited lands of the world! Or that Japan, possessed of two-thirds the population of this nation and a military organization fifty-fold greater, shall continue to exist on her rocky isles that are, inclusive of Korea, but one-two-hundred-and-fiftieth of the earth's lands,

[63]

while an undefended one-half lies under the guns of her battleships!

.   .   .   .

"The Monroe Doctrine is Promethean in conception, but not so in execution. It was proclaimed in order to avoid wars; now it invites them. . . .

"The Monroe Doctrine, if not supported by naval and military power sufficient to enforce its observance by all nations, singly and in coalition, becomes a factor more provocative of war than any other national policy ever attempted in modern or ancient times. . . . Societies, religions, unions, business men, and politicians on the one hand, spare no effort to debase every militant instinct and military efficiency or preparation necessary for its enforcement, while, on the other, they demand that the Chief Executive shall assert to the entire world this Republic's intention to maintain, by the force of arms if necessary, this most warlike and encompassing policy ever enunciated by man or nation."

The Monroe Doctrine did not require that any American possessions of the European monarchies should be relinquished, but simply that they should not be extended; and that, if relinquished or lost, they should not be re-established as monarchical possessions.

England, being in possession of the vast domain

of Canada in North America, British Honduras and British Guiana in South America, and a goodly number of the West Indian islands, was in a position to look with favor on the Monroe Doctrine, because in the event of Great Britain being defeated in war by any of the Great Powers, her victor or victors would be unable to seize any of her American possessions, for automatically the United States would become an ally of Great Britain, and would, in order to defend the Monroe Doctrine, have to defend these possessions.

When Sir Charles Tupper was High Commissioner of Canada, the writer saw him in London, and suggested to him that it would be a good idea for the Canadians to buy some automatic guns. He replied that Canada was very peculiarly situated; that she could not be attacked successfully by any Power unless the British fleet were first destroyed, which was not likely, and, in the possible event of that fleet being destroyed, then the United States would be obliged to defend Canada in order to defend the Monroe Doctrine.

The peace sophists often refer to the unfortified border-line between the United States and Canada as an argument in favor of the abolition of armaments throughout the world. They fail to perceive that the same unarmed condition would not work between European countries, as, for example, between France and Germany. If the people of Canada and the United States were as

different in race, language, ideals, and ambitions
as are the French and Germans; and if, also, the
two countries were as thickly settled and the inhabitants as land-hungry; and if each had a history as antagonistic as the French and Germans;
then fortifications would be needed on the Cana-
dian border. But the Canadians and ourselves
are of the same race, we speak the same tongue,
we have similar ideals and ambitions, and our
history is not antagonistic; on the contrary, it has
been largely a common history—the history of
England, the mother country.

England and France were obligated to defend
Belgium against Germany. Their defenses consisted mainly in bluff, but they were, nevertheless,
far better prepared to support Belgium than we
would be to support any South American country
against German aggression.

The navy of England is so far superior to ours
that should she at any time care to ignore the
Monroe Doctrine and colonize in South America
we should be absolutely unable to prevent her.
She would be able to isolate us from South America and from the rest of the world, within the
continental territory of the forty-eight states. An
impenetrable barrier of British warships would lie
between us and the Panama Canal. Therefore,
it will be seen that our Monroe Doctrine is an
Anglo-American compact, an *entente,* which we
are obliged to defend if it should be in the interest

of Great Britain, and which Great Britain would not be obliged to observe in case she might want to ignore it:

Let us invite Admiral Mahan to conclude this chapter:

"In the Monroe Doctrine, as now understood, and viewed in the light of the Venezuela incident, with the utterances then made by our statesmen of all parties, we have on hand one of the biggest contracts any modern state has undertaken."

CHAPTER IV

MODERN METHODS AND MACHINERY OF WAR

"In the course of time, no one knows when or how soon, the family of nations may get to playing at cards, and beyond the sea, perhaps, will be found a 'full hand' against our three 'aces' —the Navy, Coast Fortifications, and the Militia."

Lieut. Gen. Adna R. Chaffee, U.S.A.

"Whenever a nation's attitude toward war is evasive, its conduct indecisive, and its preparation an indifferent, orderless assembling of forces, it prepares for defeat."

Homer Lea.

IN the *Sunday American* of the seventeenth of January of this year, Mr. Andrew Carnegie gave expression to some opinions that challenge the attention of all thinking people of our country who, in this trying time of war, are becoming aroused and are asking themselves the question: Are we adequately prepared against the dread eventuality of war, and if not adequately prepared, why not?

There is no person, of howsoever humble a station, whose opinion has not some weight. Horace Greeley—or was it Henry Ward Beecher? —once said that his views upon a very important subject underwent a material change from conver-

[68]

sation with a blacksmith while having his horse shod.

The opinion of Andrew Carnegie, the greatest steel and iron smith the world has ever known, is certain to have great weight with a very large number of persons, whatever the subject may be upon which he expresses himself.

The world owes Andrew Carnegie a debt of deep gratitude for many most munificent and beneficent actions, and our gratitude to him has begotten love for him, and our gratitude and our love beget our sympathetic attention whenever he speaks. Consequently, when Mr. Carnegie speaks upon the subject of our national defense, he is bound to exercise a tremendous power for good or evil, and this power for good or evil is directly proportionate to the extent that his opinions are right or wrong.

At this time, the question of our national defense is one of so serious concern that anything a well and favorably known man says may have a determining effect upon the minds of many persons, and thereby be fruitful of national good or national harm.

If Mr. Carnegie is right in his belief that our best defense is in military defenselessness, then he is doing the country a great service through the wide publicity given to his opinions. If, on the other hand, he is in the wrong, he is doing this country a very great injury, and his words not only help defeat Congressional appropriations for building more guns, but also help to spike the few guns we have.

Let us first consider some of the more remarkable and also the more radical of his statements. He says, to quote:

"Not one of the great nations has the slightest desire to be other than friendly with the United States. We are a friend to all; an enemy of none. They could gain nothing by a war with us, nor would we by a war with them. We have no territorial ambitions, and only desire to be left alone.

"As for this foolish talk of an invasion, that is an impossible contingency. Imagine any country being able to successfully bring enough troops to accomplish anything worth while from a military standpoint from a point three thousand miles off and attack a hundred millions of people!

"I have always said that if at any time any country was foolish enough to attempt invasion the best possible plan would be to make their landing as easy as possible, point out to them the best possible roads, and allow them to go as far as they desired to go inland. Then warn them to look out, and turn a million of our 16,000,000 of militia loose upon them. Getting in would be easy, but how to get out would result in surrender.

"There is no other country in the world so well

*equipped to repel invasion or make it so hot for an
enemy should he land as to make him exceedingly
sorry he ever tried it."*

The foregoing statements of Mr. Carnegie con-
tain in a nutshell the whole pith and gist of the
present anti-armament peace advocacy, backed by
the ten-million-dollar Carnegie foundation, repre-
senting an income of half a million dollars a year.

Now, if it happens to be a fact that these views
of Mr. Carnegie and his coterie of peace advocates are wrong, and if we need to take immediate
and radical measures for our national defense,
then whenever the Carnegie advocacy prevents a
battery of guns being built, the resultant injury
to the country is as great as though a battery of
our guns were to be destroyed, or as though a battery of guns were made for a possible enemy.

Truly, as Mr. Carnegie states, we are friendly
to other nations, and we do not want any of their
territory, but I do not agree with him that we have
nothing which they might want, for we are both
very rich and very defenseless, and the history
of nations has shown that always the rich and
the defenseless sooner or later become the prey
of the poor and the powerful.

One after another of the surrounding nations
will likely be drawn into the war before it is over.
After the present belligerents have settled their
scores with the sword, there will be other scores

to be settled between the victors and the neutral nations. Differences between the warring and the neutral powers—differences which, in time of peace, might produce very strained relations or precipitate war—may now be lightly passed over as mere discourtesies. But, after the war, some of the acts of the neutrals that at present seem quite insignificant may be magnified to advantage as *casus belli*.

It is my opinion that, whichever side wins, the United States will likely have to fight the winner within a short time after the war is over, for neither the Germans nor the Allies, in the heat of passion that now dominates them, will be in a mood to forgive some of the things that we may feel compelled to do in the maintenance of our neutrality. In short, the things that we may be led to do to avoid being embroiled in the present war may serve to embroil us with the victors, unless the war should end in a draw.

Mr. Carnegie thinks it would be quite a difficult undertaking for a foreign nation to land troops enough on our shores successfully to contend with our people. Our expert army and navy officers, who have been educated at government expense, and who are supposed to know about such matters, tell us that it would be impossible for us to mobilize and bring to the front more than 30,000 of our standing Army during the first month; and that it would be impossible to mobilize and get our militia into shape to resist an army of 100,000 of the well-trained and well-armed troops of one of the Great Powers, inside of a year and a half.

Also, our naval and military experts tell us that it would require not only months, but years, to get our Navy into such efficient fighting trim as to be able to resist the navy of any one of the leading Great Powers of the world. They tell us that we are so short of ammunition that we might easily exhaust the present supply in the first four weeks of the war, and possibly in the first few days of the war.

We are in the habit of speaking of our Navy as ranking somewhere second or third from the top. As a matter of fact, we rank much lower than that, because of the shortage of our ammunition supply. Just as a steam-engine cannot be run without fuel, regardless of its size and power, so a navy cannot be run without gunpowder.

When the present war broke out, France, Germany, and England each had ten times as much smokeless powder on hand as we had. We have between forty and fifty million pounds of smokeless powder at the present time, whereas we should have 500,000,000 pounds.

The only difficulty in landing as large an army as an enemy might desire upon our shore, would be in overcoming our fleet. Once our fleet were smashed, an enemy could land a hundred thousand men, either on our Atlantic or on our Pacific seaboard, long before we could mobilize the troops we have. In fact, a quarter of a million men could be landed before we could get the troops we have into fighting shape.

Let us examine for one moment Mr. Carnegie's proposition to welcome an army of invaders, showing them the best roads to the interior, and then turning lose on them a million improvised citizen soldiers. Like Pompey, Mr. Carnegie seems to believe that he can raise an army at will by stamping his foot upon the ground.

Not only should we have to raise the million men, but also we should have to provide small arms, Maxim guns, rapid-fire field-cannon, and siege howitzers for them. At least four years' instruction and experience in the use of these weapons would be required; furthermore, the men would have to be imbued with the courage that veterans have, which can be acquired only after much experience on the firing-line; they would have to be officered by men of military education and training, and lastly, they would need large corps of trained and experienced engineers, and also a trained commissariat.

None of these things can be created in a day, or a month, or made efficient in a year, so that the army of invaders, after it had received the Carnegie welcome and had taken possession of the country, would have quietly to wait for us to get ready to swoop down on them, as Mr. Carnegie suggests.

When the present war is over, should one of the belligerent nations, with its veteran fighting blood up, attack us, how are we prepared to meet that attack?

Our army and navy men tell us that our position is pathetically defenseless. They tell us that, should our Navy be destroyed or evaded, and an army of only a hundred thousand men, equipped with all of the arms and paraphernalia of modern warfare, be landed on our coast, the invading army could go anywhere it might see fit, live off the country, capture our big cities, and hold us up for ransom in spite of all that we could do.

What could we do? How could we flee? Where could we flee? We simply could not flee. Most of us have doubtless thought that if war should be declared, we would seek safety in the interior. But immediately war is declared, all the railroads and all automobiles will be commandeered for military purposes. All banks will close. All securities will be rendered worthless, and we, reduced to penniless hoboes, will be compelled to stay right here and face the music.

Let us assume merely that an invading army of a hundred thousand men should be landed near New York. Should this army send out detachments to capture the places where our arms and munitions of war are made, they would not have far to go.

A Rich Prize for a Hostile Army

They would find the smokeless powder works of the United States Army and the Picatinny Arsenal, where all the smokeless powder and high explosives of the United States Army are stored, near Dover, New Jersey, about thirty-five miles from New York; also they would find there the big naval depot for ammunition and explosives.

At Bridgeport, Connecticut, they would find the Union Metallic Cartridge Works, and the American and British Manufacturing Company's Works for the manufacture of rapid-fire cannon, and at New Haven they would find the Winchester Repeating Arms and Cartridge Company's Works and the Marlin Firearms Works. At Springfield, Massachusetts, they would find the Smith and Wesson Revolver Works and also the United States Arsenal, where our rifles are made. At Hartford, Connecticut, they would find the Colt Patent Firearms, and the Pratt and Whitney Works; at Ilion, New York, the Remington Small Arms Works, and at Utica, New York, the Savage Arms Works.

They would find one of our most important big-gun factories at Troy, New York, and another at Bethlehem, Pennsylvania, where also much of

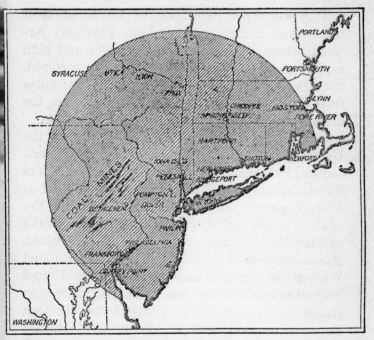

The Heart of America

Within a circle of 170 miles radius drawn around Peekskill, N. Y., are embraced New York City, Boston, Philadelphia, and many other important cities; also most of the manufactories of armaments and war materials, together with the principal coal fields of Pennsylvania

our armor-plate is made. The big Cramp Ship-building Works would be found at Philadelphia. They would find at Groton, Connecticut, the factory where all the interior parts of the Holland submarine boats are made, and at Fore River, Massachusetts, the big shipyard where the Holland submarine and other war vessels are constructed.

They would find the Lake Submarine Torpedo Boat Works at Bridgeport, the United States Naval Torpedo Station at Newport, Rhode Island, and one of our biggest navy yards, together with the E. W. Bliss Torpedo Works, in Brooklyn. The New York Arsenal they would find unprotected on Governor's Island. They would find the great duPont Smokeless Powder Works at Carney's Point, Parlin and Pompton Lakes, New Jersey, and at various points in New Jersey the largest and most important high-explosives works in the world.

Take a map of the United States, and a pair of compasses, and with one point placed on the Hudson River, at Peekskill, New York, draw a circle having a radius of a hundred-and-sixty miles. There will be included within that circle all of the above-mentioned ammunition and armament works, which constitute nearly all the smokeless powder works, cartridge works, torpedo-boat works, small-arms works, and big-gun and armor-plate works in the United States. Also, this circle will include not only New York and nearby cities, but also Boston, Albany, Syracuse, Philadelphia, and the most important coal fields of Pennsylvania.

The conquest of this area would not be a work of months, or of years, but only of a few days, and the thing would be done before we had time to mobilize the available fighting forces we have, much less to enlist and train and arm a citizen soldiery.

This vital area is the solar plexus of Uncle Sam, and an army of a hundred thousand trained men, landed on our Atlantic seaboard, would be able to capture this entire area and subdue the populace as easily as the police force of New York can subdue a rioting mob.

While we were arming and training our million men to make the Carnegie swoop, the army of invaders would be very busy.

They would commandeer all our above-mentioned factories, and proceed to operate them with skilled American labor, which they would also commandeer and force to work, just as the Germans have forced the Belgians to work for them, and Mr. Carnegie's army of citizen soldiers would find themselves without means either of arming themselves or of supplying themselves with ammunition or of getting the skilled labor necessary to do the work.

But this is not all that the invaders would be

doing while we were getting our million men together. They would have means of knowing what
we were doing, and they would send out a detach-
ment and defeat our whole enterprise. They
would probably levy on New York City for a billion dollars, and levy upon all the cities in the
captured area for every dollar that could be
squeezed from the inhabitants under threats of
destruction.

Not only this, but they might take the notion,
and probably would take the notion, to annex the
conquered territory, just as Germany has annexed
Belgium, and, as we should then automatically
become citizens of the enemy's country, we should
be conscripted and forced to fight our own people,
just as the Belgians, according to report, have
been forced into the ranks of the Germans.

Such a military measure is not new; it is as old
as war itself. Frederick the Great frequently
forced his prisoners to fight in his own ranks, and
Napoleon Bonaparte sometimes gave them the
option of joining his legions or of faring much
worse. Attila took with him the entire male population of the countries through which he passed as
additions to his military host. Those who resisted were immediately killed, and those he did
not need were killed, whether they resisted or not.
As to what may be done in war, there is no arbiter
but necessity.

To receive an invading army is not so pleasant a

thing as Mr. Carnegie assumes. As guests they are just about as lovable and make just about as good pets in the family as rattlesnakes, cobras, scorpions, and tarantulas.

A few Americans who were caught in the war zone when the present war broke out got some useful knowledge of war's inconveniences and harassments. What the people for whom there was no escape suffered in Belgium and Northern France, is beyond our powers of conception. No one who has not had personal experience can form the least idea of the barbarous atrocities perpetrated by an invading army on the defenseless population.

Invaders always live off the invaded country. It is considered more important that they should live well than that any one else should live at all. If, after the invaders' wants are supplied, there is enough left for the people to live on, well and good; if not, then the people must starve. The invaders must have food and clothing and the bare necessaries of life; also, they must have luxuries. They must have cigars and cigarettes, wine, women, and song. If our country should be invaded, we should not only have to furnish food, clothing, cigars, cigarettes, and wine for the armies of the enemy, but also our wives and our daughters and our sweethearts would be commandeered to supply the women and song.

Occasionally, an American citizen, with more

manhood than discretion, would resent a nameless indignity, and kill some military blackguard, who would immediately be avenged by the burning of the town and the corralling and shooting of the people with machine-guns. This is not an overdrawn picture—the thing has actually been done in the present war.

It is very likely that some of us who look upon this page will be forced to see wife or daughter or sweetheart namelessly maltreated to gratify the brutal lust of an invader, and lose our own life for a blow on the scoundrel's jaw or a stab in his ribs, unless—aye, there's the rub—unless this whole country awakens to its danger and rises up as one man and demands prompt and adequate defensive measures for national protection. As this saving thing is not likely to happen, the entire country east of the Alleghanies will probably be Belgiumized with fire and the sword, depredated, degraded, and desolated by an invading army within a very short time after the European War is over.

This is an age of mechanics—an age wherein man-made mechanism more and more replaces hand work. Everywhere in our industries of peace, we have seen labor-saving machinery replace the labor of human hands. Today all the men in the world could not do by hand all of the world's ploughing, sowing, reaping, and carrying of the world's food to market; all the women in the world could not, today, do the world's sewing without the sewing-machine; and all the men in the world and all the women in the world combined could not, today, do a tenth of the world's writing without the typewriter and type-setting and printing machinery.

One of the giant dredges that have been ladling out of the Panama Canal the vast landslides, can do the pick and shovel and wheelbarrow work of a thousand men. Everywhere, in everything we do, and in everything done for us, we find human hands now mainly engaged in guiding the work of labor-saving machinery.

The people of the United States of America have been able to develop their enormous resources and to keep abreast of the world's industrial progress mainly by the invention of labor-saving machinery under the protection of our patent law.

In our competition with other nations for the markets of the world, no one thinks of referring to the prowess of our unskilled citizen soldiers of industry unsupported by machinery, but all reliance is placed upon our multiform labor-saving machinery, and our skilled labor behind that machinery.

With these pregnant facts before us, it is very strange that it should not be perfectly plain to every one that what is true of labor-saving machinery in peace is likewise true in war. It is very strange indeed that there should be intelligent men and women among us unable to see and to understand that labor-saving machinery and labor skilled in its use are as applicable and as indispensable to successful warfare as to peaceful industry. Furthermore, labor-saving machinery in war is life-saving machinery. The quick-firing gun is the greatest life-saving instrument ever invented. These persons do not seem to appreciate that war is an industry. As a matter of stern fact, war is, and has always been, the biggest and the most vital industry of mankind, and in no other industry is labor-saving machinery so important and so vital, and in no other industry does so much depend upon the skill of the labor operating the machinery.

We are the slaves of belief, and we love our chains. Although our faith may be false, we hate the hand that tries to free us. The people of this country have a great false faith in the fighting qualities of their citizen soldiery, improvised in time of war. They point proudly to the War of the Revolution and the War of the Rebellion to prove how our volunteer soldiers can fight. They overlook the fact that fighting was then mostly done by hand; that now it is mostly done by machinery, and that it is just as foolish and absurd to think of taking untrained men off the farm to operate the guns and machinery of war as it would be to try to operate the factories with them where the guns and machinery are made. It takes as long today to convert a farmer into a skilled soldier as it does to convert him into a skilled mechanic.

Battles are no longer decided merely by the patriotism and personal bravery of the rank and file, nor even by their numbers, but by the efficiency and sufficiency of machinery and materials of destruction and the science and scientific experience of the commanding officers. There is no time to build steam-fire-engines or to train fire brigades after a conflagration has broken out.

A citizen soldiery without years of training in the discipline and weapons and mechanism of modern warfare is only a mob, as easily scattered by a few real soldiers as chaff by a whirlwind.

George Washington held the following opinion about the value of militia in warfare:

"Regular troops alone are equal to the exigencies of modern war, as well for defense as offense, and when a substitute is attempted it must prove illusory and ruinous. No militia will ever acquire the habits necessary to resist a regular force . . . the firmness requisite for the real business of fighting is only to be attained by a constant course of discipline and service. I have never yet been witness to a single instance that can justify a different opinion, and it is most earnestly to be

wished that the liberties of America may no longer be trusted, in any material degree, to so precarious a dependence."—Washington.

If Washington held it a mistake to rely on untrained, undisciplined men in time of war, who can differ with him today, when not only bravery and discipline are required, but also a knowledge of the complicated enginery of warfare?

It is obvious to any one that ten men armed with the modern magazine shoulder-rifle, with a range of more than two miles, would easily be able to defeat a thousand men—a hundred times their number—armed with slings and bows and arrows, short-swords and spears, as was the army of Hannibal. Hannibal's famous Balearic slingers were able to hurl a slug of lead through a man. But ten riflemen would have time to kill a thousand of them before they could get within sling range. A thousand of the famous English bowmen who fought at Agincourt could all be destroyed by our ten riflemen before they could get within bowshot.

The same thing holds equally true with old short-range and obsolete firearms, as compared with the longer range and more accurate guns of the latest pattern. Ten good marksmen, armed with the latest rifles, could kill a thousand equally skilled marksmen armed with the old muzzle-loaders of the Civil War, before they could get within range. These ten men would each be able to fire with ease a carefully aimed shot every two and a half seconds; the ten men could fire 250 aimed shots a minute. A thousand men, armed with the old muzzle-loaders, would surely have to advance at least a mile and a half after coming within range of the modern rifles before they could get the ten riflemen within range of their muzzle-loaders. Charging forward on the run, it would take them at least ten minutes to cover the mile and a half. In that time the ten riflemen would be able to fire 2,500 carefully-aimed shots. Such is the difference in the potentiality of troops dependent upon suitable arms.

With the modern automatic magazine-rifle a single soldier would be able to defeat a hundred men armed with the old smooth-bore single-shot muzzle-loaders of the Civil War; in fact, he would be able to kill or wound every one of them in an open frontal attack over level ground with his long-range rapid-fire rifle before they could get near enough even to reach him with their short-range muskets. One man operating an automatic machine-gun would be more than a match for a thousand men, armed with the old Civil War musket in an open-view frontal attack, over a distance covered by the range of the machine gun. In fact, with this weapon, firing 600 shots a minute, he could play the gun on their advancing line with the freedom of a hose pipe, and put them *hors de combat* in a few minutes—certainly, before they could get near enough to reach him with their short-range guns.

Half a dozen automatic machine-guns supported by a battery of half a dozen modern rapid-fire field-guns throwing shrapnel shell at the rate of from thirty to forty a minute, planted on Cemetery Hill, would have been able to defeat Pickett's charge at Gettysburg more quickly than did the entire Army of the Potomac.

It is obvious, therefore, that a nation's war potentiality depends very largely upon its preparedness to fight by machinery, and that a mere citizen soldiery, without the machinery of modern warfare, is as impotent in the face of modern war engines as a swarm of ants in the face of an ant-eater. It is obvious that, whereas fighting machinery is very expensive, modern warfare is a very costly business, and a business requiring an enormous investment; and also that, whereas a thing is worth most in war which can, for the least cost, produce the best results, machinery becomes much more valuable than life. A single field-piece may be worth more than a hundred men, and at times even more than a thousand men.

In modern warfare, the cost in treasure and machinery is of far greater concern than the loss in blood. Therefore, the efficiency and great cost of all kinds of modern fighting equipment have served to give the great nations pause, and to make them consider well the awful risk before precipitating war. The progress in fighting machinery of every sort has been so rapid, and the number of wars so few, that until now there has been no adequate opportunity to test fighting machinery in actual warfare.

In direct proportion as warfare becomes more scientific, complicated, and expensive does it require longer time to prepare for war, both in the making of the enginery and in the making of the soldiers.

Time signifies only the measure of change. Consequently, time is merely a relative term, indicative of the sequence in a series of happenings or eventuations. If the universe were annihilated, there would be no such thing as time because nothing would happen.

Were we to be attacked by any foreign Power, we should be able to rely, not upon what we might be able to produce three or four years afterward, but upon what we should be able to put into action at once. Modern methods and machinery of war cause events to move many times as fast as in former wars. Three months is a long time after war is declared. A six months' war today is relatively as long as a six years' war used to be.

The following extract from Bernhardi's "How Germany Makes War" is evidence of that expert's opinion of the factor of time:

"If Germany is involved in war, she need not recoil before the numerical superiority of her enemies. But so far as human nature is able to tell, she can only rely on being successful if she is resolutely determined to break the superiority of her enemies by a victory over one or the other of them before their total strength can come into action, and if she prepares for war to that effect, and acts at the decisive moment in that spirit which made Frederick the Great seize the sword against a world in arms."

Napoleon once said, "The fate of nations often hangs on five minutes," and, "God fights on the side of the heaviest artillery." Also, he said, in effect, that the art of winning battles depends upon the concentration on the chief point of attack of a force superior to the enemy at that point.

If we pass our finger down the pages of history, we shall find the above expression of Napoleon thoroughly substantiated and vindicated. Most great battles have been won by the concentration of a superior force upon an inferior force at some vulnerable point, and often quite irrespective of the sizes of the opposing armies taken as a whole. Everything depends upon the quickness in concentration of concerted action. The herculean physique of Goliath did not count for much after little David hit him with the pebble. He needs be a big man indeed not to be whipped when even a small antagonist has succeeded in thrusting a dagger close to the heart. Armies, like individuals, have vital parts, the penetration of which means defeat.

Alexander the Great frequently met and annihilated armies many times larger than his own. He was often weaker than the enemy as a whole, but at the point of attack he was always vastly the stronger. This enabled him to crush the enemy in detail. Hannibal, Cæsar, Charles Martel, Marlborough, Cromwell, Frederick the Great, Napoleon, Grant, Lee, Stonewall Jackson, Sheridan —all great captains—appreciated and applied this winning principle: Be able to strike the enemy upon one given point with greater force than he shall be able to oppose, and strike first; then follow up the advantage and crush the enemy in detail by concentrated force always superior at the point of attack, however inferior to the general force to which it is opposed and through which it penetrates.

Broadly speaking, the machinery of modern warfare adds a thousand-fold to the potentiality of the soldier in battle above his potentiality at the time of the Civil War.

Ten thousand men, armed with modern guns and all the paraphernalia of modern warfare, would on the battle-line be more than a match for a million men armed with the old smooth-bore guns of the Civil War. As a matter of fact they could kill all that surrounded them as fast as they approached from every quarter, and they could advance through the opposing lines with absolute freedom without the loss of a single man from the fire of the enemy.

Let us see for one moment what ten thousand men would be able to do upon such a host in open frontal attack: Let us assume that the ten thousand were armed with a thousand automatic guns, and, say, a hundred rapid-fire field-guns, in addition to the usual magazine shoulder-rifle. As soon as the enemy came in sight, the ten thousand would open on them with their hundred field-guns, pouring into their ranks a perfect storm of shrapnel. The old, smooth-bore field-guns of the enemy would be completely disabled before they could be brought within cannon-shot of the ten thousand. As soon as the enemy came within rifle range, the ten thousand would open on them with their thousand automatic machine-guns and magazine-rifles. As an automatic machine-gun fires at the rate of 600 shots a minute, a thousand would fire at the rate of 600,000 shots a minute. The magazine shoulder-rifles would fire aimed shots at the rate of twenty-five a minute, and the quick-firing field-guns would each fire shrapnel at the rate of forty a minute. Making every allowance for stoppages and for variables, dispersion of fire and bad marksmanship, there would be enough ef-fectual hits with the shrapnel, the automatic ma-

chine-gun fire, and the magazine-rifle fire, to kill
or wound every man of the enemy before that
enemy could get near enough to reach the ten
thousand with their old smooth-bore muskets.

Every automatic gun and every quick-firing
field-gun and every magazine shoulder-rifle puts
in the hands of our soldiers the means of avoiding
a corresponding sacrifice of their lives. Not only
this, but every automatic gun that we make and
furnish our troops enables one man to do the
work of a hundred men; it enables a hundred
men to remain at home engaged in peaceful pursuits while only one man has to go to the battle
front and fight.

Then let us realize the fact that every automatic
gun saves a hundred lives from jeopardy. Every
magazine-rifle saves ten lives, and every quick-
firing field-cannon saves easily a hundred lives.

This should make a strong appeal to the professional pacifists who pretend that they want to
save life. Surely, if war cannot be prevented,
and all history, and the present moment as well,
prove that it cannot, then we should make it as
merciful as possible, and fight it in a way that will
cause as little sacrifice of life as possible.

In estimating the cost of war in human lives, we
cannot count values that may be placed upon them
by sentiments of humanity, but only such values
as, when destroyed, make the losing nation economically so much the poorer.

According to I. S. Bloch, a new-born child of the farming class has a value of twenty-five dollars. At five years of age, he has a value of two hundred and fifty dollars; at ten years of age, he is worth about five hundred dollars; at fifteen, he is worth almost a thousand dollars; and at twenty, he is worth a little more than a thousand dollars. His maximum value is at twenty, and he begins to depreciate in value as he grows older, because of his shortened days of service.

Therefore, the average economic value of soldiers may, according to Mr. Bloch, be put at a thousand dollars.

According to David Starr Jordan, it costs about fifteen thousand dollars for each soldier killed in battle, so that, according to these two eminent peace advocates and peace propagandists, when the Germans slay, say, a thousand of the Allies, the loss to the Allies is the value of the thousand men, namely, a million dollars, and as it costs the Germans fifteen times as much to kill them as they are worth, the loss to the Germans is fifteen million dollars; so that the actual German loss is fifteen times as great as that of the Allies. But as the Allies are killing a good many Germans, they are generously sharing with the Germans a fair proportion of the cost of the war.

These figures are not far out of the way. The fact is that, in modern warfare, the actual loss of life for the numbers engaged is correspondingly less than it used to be, while the cost is correspondingly greater. In modern warfare, the loss of money is far greater than the loss of life. It is more the dollar than blood, that is now shed.

In ancient times, when men fought hand to hand in compact form, with short-sword, spear, and battle-axe, they used often to slay half the numbers engaged—easily ten times as many for the numbers engaged as are now slain. There are more than ten million Allies now under arms against more than seven million Germans and Austrians. These numbers have not as yet all been brought face to face with one another on the line of battle, owing to modern methods of warfare; but under old-time methods with old-time arms, they would have been at once brought into collision in two enormous armies. In ancient times, less mobilization could be effected in a year than can now be effected in a month, but when the collision came, the issue of the war was decided on one great field.

If these great European armies were armed with short-swords, spears, and battle-axes, as armies used to be, instead of with modern war weapons and enginery, they would, during the time they have been engaged, very likely have slain a third of their number—certainly ten times as many in proportion to the numbers engaged as have actually been killed in the present war.

Even a tenth of their numbers would be a million and a half.

Never in all history have such vast numbers of men been drawn up in line of battle. Never have they been so scientifically armed, and, consequently, never have they, for the numbers engaged, killed so few.

Modern machine-guns and quick-firing guns, with bullets and shrapnel and canister, are so deadly that troops in mass form cannot live for a minute in front of them, but as opposing armies with modern war machinery line up at the present greater tactical distances, and throw out their men in long-extended battle-lines, and spread them over correspondingly wide areas, the fight becomes one largely of gun against gun, engine against engine, with the result that not nearly so many lives are lost as there would be if the fighting were done by hand, and hand to hand, in close order. The German siege guns smashed the forts of Liège and Namur from a distance of nine miles.

As nations are bound to fight, it is far more merciful that they should be armed to the teeth, but it is vastly more expensive. Can we not afford, however, to spend dollars instead of men to kill our enemies?

Therefore, even according to the facts and figures of those two eminent peace-men, I. S. Bloch and Dr. David Starr Jordan, the money loss today is a concern fifteen times more serious to the economic welfare of a nation than is the loss in lives.

It is a very strange paradox indeed that the professional peace-propagandists, who claim to be actuated mainly by considerations of humanity, should advocate disarmament and the inevitable reversion to the old and more deadly arms and methods of warfare, on account of the greater expensiveness of warfare conducted with modern scientific arms and methods.

By doing away with our present highly scientific and very expensive war enginery and fighting methods, the nations would be able, in a war like the present, to kill one another at very much less cost. They would then be able to kill ten times as many in a given time, while the cost would be only a small fraction of the present cost.

It is a matter of solemn certainty that the quick-firing gun is the most beneficent implement of mercy that has ever been invented, and every peace advocate in the world and every lover of his kind should appreciate this fact and use his influence in favor of armaments which serve to make war expensive, and tend both to prevent war, and to save life when war comes.

Let us for a moment suppose that the great European Powers had disarmed fifteen years ago when the Czar of Russia broached the subject to them. What would have been the result? This war would have come just the same, and probably much sooner; and it would have been ten-fold more bloody, even had the nations flung themselves upon one another armed with scythes, carving-knives, wood-axes, and common tools of trade, or even had they fought, as the simple cave men did, with clubs and stones.

Love of home and country—patriotism—on the one hand, and race hatred on the other, are far more potent in the human heart than any lately created sentiments of international brotherhood and humanity. Before this war came, it was a common preachment of the peace-men and a common belief of the multitude, that many socialists, members of brotherhoods of labor and other opponents of war, would refuse to fight, and if drafted would shoot down their officers from the rear. But nothing of this kind has happened. When this war broke out, socialist, labor unionist, and preacher of international brotherhood joined with their militant fellow-countrymen in singing the "Marseillaise," "Wacht am Rhein," "Britannia Rules the Waves," and rushed to arms and to war, and are now fighting like demons, shoulder to shoulder with the imperialist and the war lord.

In order that we may be made as right-seeking as possible, God has ordained the trials of strife and hardship which force us to get busy, and thereby develop our usefulness. Human duty may be expressed in the following terms: The best preparation for the attainment of success in life is the acquisition of a thorough realization of the fact that no one deserves more from the world than he earns out of it, and that the bigness or littleness of any one is exactly proportionate to his use to the world, and that, consequently, actual self-service is impossible except indirectly through world-service.

Whatever may be done in the service of an individual to help him attain success and find comfort, or to lessen his discomfort, may not be best for the general good, because individual welfare must, in the end of things, be subservient to the general welfare.

It sometimes becomes perfectly right and proper that individual life should be sacrificed for national life, but never national life for individual life. The nation has, however, its obligations to the individual, and obligations as exacting as those of the individual to the nation. If a nation does not exercise due and reasonable diligence to safeguard its people against war and does not provide itself with the necessary trained men and machinery to forefend war, then the obligation of the individual to the nation in the event of war is just so much lessened. The leading of an untrained and ill-armed, improvised citizen soldiery against an army of trained veterans, with all of the equipment of modern warfare, results in useless, senseless slaughter.

If a nation does not prepare itself to demand and enforce respectful treatment of its citizens in foreign countries, then its citizens should have no patriotism, for they are like men and women without a country. But when a nation is armed with guns, and armed with the purpose to defend its citizens, wherever they may be, to the last man and last pinch of gunpowder, and is so adequately prepared with labor-saving, life-saving machinery that in the event of war the minimum of human sacrifice shall be made, then it is the duty of every man to place himself unreservedly at the service of his country.

If the people of this country could be roused to a realization of what invasion means, there would be no longer heard any senseless prating about an unarmed peace, but the whole people would rise in their might and demand adequate armaments and an adequate army and navy, and the senseless peace fanatics would be burned in effigy.

We have for half a century listened with confidence to the assurance that we are so splendidly isolated by broad seas that we need not fear invasion.

Our inadequate Navy is today the only bulwark against invasion, for modern means of transportation over seas have reduced the ocean to a ferry.

Both England and Germany have navies superior to our own, and would be able to destroy our Navy, and land on our unfortified shores a

hundred thousand men in less than two weeks—
half the time that would be required for us to
mobilize our little Army of thirty thousand men.

Japan is not so far away as she used to be. She
has been rapidly narrowing the Pacific, and she
could land a quarter of a million men on the Pacific coast in less than a month, much quicker
than we could get our thirty thousand regulars
there to receive them.

We are no longer splendidly isolated from other
nations. We are isolated only from ourselves,
and we are truly splendidly isolated in that particular.

The other nations are isolated only by such
time and difficulty as they would have to encounter
in order to bring veteran troops to our shores,
with all the necessary equipment of war, and, as
we have seen, this is an isolation of less than a
month, while we are isolated by unpreparedness
by at least fifty months, for it would take more
than four years, if we should start now, to raise,
equip, and train an army that would compare in
numbers, equipment, and training with the army
that any one of the Great Powers could place upon
our shores in a month.

In a recent interview, Secretary of War Garrison said:

*"If tomorrow any first-class military power
should attack the United States in force and*

[100]

*should succeed in getting her warships and sol-
dier-laden transports past our fleet, landed out of
range of our coast defenses, once fairly ashore she
could pulverize our small regular army and punish
us to a humiliating degree, if not actually make us
sue for peace, before we could raise and train a
volunteer army adequate to cope with the invaders. In other words, at present our navy is
our only considerable bulwark against invasion.
Even such part of our militia as we could depend
on and the available regular army would make an
extremely small force, our army being in size only
a local police force, well trained and highly efficient indeed, but in numbers little more than twice
the size of the police force of New York City—
that is, not large enough for our great country
even as a mere police force."*

Let us, for argument's sake, assume for a moment that we were to be invaded with an army of
only a hundred thousand men, trained, equipped,
and supplied with the supreme adequacy with
which the troops of the other Great Powers are
trained, equipped, and supplied.

The enemy would line up in a battle-front three
times as long as our little thirty thousand could
be stretched with equal powers of concentration,
or if our thirty thousand were to be stretched
out a hundred miles we should be at least
three times as weak as the enemy at any point

of attack, even were our thirty thousand to be as well equipped and as well supplied as the troops of the enemy. But we should be without the requisite field artillery, and the artillery that we should have would be without the requisite training. We should be without the needed cavalry, and our cavalry would be without proper organization and experience. We should be without ammunition trains, and very short of ammunition. Our troops, hustled together, and rushed to the front for the first time to face a real enemy, would be unprepared to behave like an army, and, what is very important, they would have no hope of success.

Despair would be in the heart of every man. Both officers and men would know that there were no ready resources, no reserves and reserve supplies behind them, and no adequate arrangements for providing any. Every man of the thirty thousand would know that he was being sacrificed in atonement for national blundering, just as at Balaklava the noble Six Hundred were by a blunder sacrificed in the charge of the Light Brigade.

PREPONDERANCE OF GUN-FIRE

It is strange how little the law of battles is understood by most persons. Most persons imagine that in a fight between our Navy and another navy, or between our Army and the army of an enemy, although the enemy might have the advantage in the number of ships and in the size and range of guns, the advantage would be immaterial and one which might be balanced by the superiority of our personnel, and that, although we might be somewhat short of the required field batteries and ammunition, the superior fighting qualities of our men would render them more than a match for the enemy, even in the face of superior gun-fire.

It does not appear to have been fully recognized even by the advocates of better equipment for the American Army, how vitally important is length of range in field artillery.

In the Boer War, the British field batteries found themselves at great disadvantage in face of the longer French guns of the Boer batteries.

In the present European war, the great long-range German howitzers, pummeling forts into heaps of scrap, and their plunging fire blowing great craters along the battle-front, spread terror in the ranks of the Allies, similar to the terror that the Romans felt when the fierce Gothic giants slid down the Alps into the vineyards of Italy. But the long-range French field-artillery soon restored confidence, for it was found that the French field batteries could outrange the German batteries.

We need field-guns of longer range. We need

field-guns that shall not only equal in range those now in use in Europe, but also we need guns of even longer range. We should have field-guns of a range sufficient to command sky-line from opposing sky-line. Here is an opportunity for the vaunted American genius to assert itself.

It is necessary that the facts as they actually are should be recognized and appreciated.

Victory in a naval battle today depends absolutely upon the weight of the broadsides and the speed of the vessels, which enables them to manœuvre and choose positions of advantage with respect to the enemy; while victory or defeat in a land fight depends upon the weight of gun-fire, which can be directed against the positions of an enemy.

The actual number of infantry engaged is of secondary importance. It is artillery that is of supreme importance. Should we be involved, our field artillery must pave the way with the dead bodies of the enemy before our infantry can advance. Also, the batteries of the enemy must be silenced by our own batteries before they, with their gun-fire, shall be able to silence ours. Other things being equal, therefore, it is the number of field batteries that, more than anything else, turns the tide of battle for defeat or victory. If the enemy's guns have a longer range than ours, then they will be able to silence our batteries while far beyond the range of our guns. They will be

Relative Numerical Strength of Field Artillery

Russia, 6,000

Germany, 5,000

France, 4,800

Austria, 2,365

Italy, 1,500

Japan, 1,250

England, 1,000

United States, 654

able to destroy our artillery, while we should not be able even to injure theirs.

Let us picture a land fight:

Our aërial scouts inform us that the enemy is approaching, and that they have already mounted their long-range field artillery on a convenient ridge; also that they have placed their big howitzers on an adjoining lowland under the concealment of a wood, and that this formation is repeated in similar units from ridge to ridge and hill to hill over a front a hundred miles in length.

The enemy has also dug long lines of trenches far in advance of their artillery. The enemy's position is well beyond the range of our artillery. We are unable to reach the enemy's position with our guns, while the enemy, being provided with guns of much longer range, is able to storm our position along our entire front, and to throw shrapnel shell into the trenches filled with our men, which stretch along the lowland in front of our positions. We try to dig additional trenches to advance our front, but the men sent to do the work are very quickly killed by the shrapnel fire of the enemy.

We see with our field-glasses that the enemy has sent out detachments to advance the line of their trenches. We fire at them, and find that our shrapnel falls far short. The enemy, seeing this, advances and digs trenches close up to the limit of the range of our guns.

All at once, the enemy opens fire with shrapnel upon our entire line of trenches, and with shrapnel and howitzers upon all our fortified positions. We return the fire, but without any effect; the range of our guns being too short to reach the enemy. Many of our guns are quickly silenced. The perfect hurricane of shrapnel thrown upon our trenches has killed large numbers of our men and confounded the remainder.

The infantry of the enemy now advances pell-mell over the intervening space, still under cover of artillery fire. Field batteries of the enemy also advance rapidly and take up new positions.

Finding our positions untenable, our army retreats precipitately, taking with it a few remaining guns, and our men re-form their batteries on commanding positions to cover our retreat, but they are soon dislodged by the long-range guns of the enemy. Finally, our army takes up its stand far in the rear, forming a new battle-front, which has been previously fortified.

The enemy advances, repeats the previous tactics, forming a long battle-front on commanding positions just beyond the range of our guns, and again proceeds to dislodge us, and drive us back by their long-range gun-fire.

Our loss in men and guns has been enormous. The enemy, on the contrary, has lost no guns, and but few men.

It will be seen that the enemy can very easily

proceed in this manner into the interior, and conquer the whole country without suffering very
much discomfiture, unless we have guns of as long
or longer range than the enemy has, and as many
of them, also as many skilled troops to operate
them.

Most persons imagine that infantry, armed with
the modern long-range magazine-rifles, can go
into battle, and shoot large numbers of an enemy,
and that, if the infantry is numerous and daring
enough and brave enough, they will be able to whip
the enemy without the support of field artillery.
This is a grave error. An army of a million men,
consisting entirely of infantry, armed with modern shoulder-arms, would be completely over-
matched and easily defeated by an army of 25,000
men amply equipped with modern field artillery.
The infantry would be wholly unable to get within
musket-range, because they would all be destroyed
by the shrapnel of the enemy before they could
get near enough to fire a single effective shot.

A hundred thousand English, Germans, or
Japanese, equipped with the longest and best
modern field artillery, with plenty of ammunition
and supply trains, air-scouts and engineer corps,
could, in our present defenseless condition, march
through this country as Xenophon's ten thousand
marched through ancient Persia. They could cut
their way through all opposition that we could
offer. We have neither the infantry, nor the ar-

tillery, nor the cavalry, to oppose them, and the artillery we have is of so much shorter range that at no time could we get near enough to the enemy to reach him with our guns.

If war comes between us and any of the Great Powers, the splendid young men of the country—husbands, fathers, sons, brothers, lovers—will have to go to the front and meet the invaders.

If they go forward equipped with the necessary arms, ammunition, and enginery of war, and are well trained and well officered, then they will be able not only to hold their own against the invaders, with comparatively little loss of life, but also to repel and drive out the enemy and save our land from spoliation and our homes from despoliation.

If, on the other hand, they are to be sent forward without the necessary arms, ammunition, and enginery, and without training, and incompetently or incompletely officered, as the pacifist propagandists and other sentimentalists are advising and planning that they be sent, then they will go just like lambs to the slaughter.

The zone of fire in front of the enemy's trenches will be heaped high, acres wide and miles long, with their dead bodies; and writhing, groaning, shrieking, agonized forms of the wounded will crawl over and under the dead toward the hope of safety and mercy.

Into such a hell are the hyper-sentimental peace

sophists planning to send those you most love, those to whom you most cling, and on whom you most depend; and you are aiding and abetting the crime if you believe the words of these false reasoners.

Every word you aim against necessary preparedness for war may, in the final reckoning, aim a gun at the heart of him whom you love more than all the world; and you might be able to say a word that would protect him with a gun.

That human attribute which, more than any other, distinguishes man from the brute, is imagination. Also, it is the attribute which, more than any other, differentiates the normal man from the criminal. If, in imagination, a would-be murderer could foresee the distorted face and the despairing agony of his dying victim, and could foresee the tear-streaming eyes of those mourning for him, he would, unless brazened against every feeling of pity, stay his hand. If those who, through their ignorance, false belief, or hypocrisy and desire for publicity, are planning to sacrifice the unimaginable thousands of our best young men in the bloody shambles of war, as an offering to false faith, vanity, or hypocrisy, could only foresee in imagination the long lines of manhood swept and annihilated by the withering fire of an enemy, without guns to return that fire, then possibly they might submerge personal limelight-lust for considerations of mercy.

If you believe them, and speak as they are speaking, and advise as they are advising, against adequate national defense, you should at once change your belief, and use your voice and every resource at your command in future to forefend this country and avert the great useless sacrifice.

Come, young lady reader, let us, in imagination, stand together on the firing-line: Those regiments lining up are from New York, New Jersey, Connecticut, Massachusetts. They are forming for a charge. It is the only way. Those shells, bursting among them with such deadly effect, are shrapnel from the quick-firing guns of the enemy placed just over the crest of yonder distant ridge; and those huge plunging projectiles, which throw up great inverted cones of earth, with fragments of men, are from the enemy's big howitzers, located under cover of the wood that fringes the horizon.

If we only had the necessary quick-firing field-guns and shrapnel ammunition, and the necessary field howitzers, we might dislodge or silence those deadly batteries of the enemy. At any rate, we should be able to engage them efficiently and cover the charge of our troops. We should also be able to storm that line of trenches, to the discomfiture of the enemy hidden there in vast numbers, and thus to prepare for the onset of our men. But we have neither the guns nor the ammunition.

See—the order is given. Onward they go.

Watch them, the brave fellows! Why does the front line lie down so suddenly, with a few left standing? My friend, they are not lying down; they are dead. But they are not all killed, a large number of them are wounded. They are torn in every inconceivable, horrible manner of mutilation. And look!—the other lines go down, too; some lying still, others writhing on the ground. One of those poor devils, with hands clenched in the grass and gnawing the earth, is your brother!

See—a huge howitzer shell explodes right among them. The young man whom you were to marry on his return from the war was standing on the verge of the crater when the explosion came, and he is now lying there, with both eyes blown out by the awful blast and hanging on his cheeks. There are visions of you in the blasted eyes, and there are thoughts of you in the dazed brain, and his dying breath is a whisper of your name.

Will you continue to think thoughts and speak words which may drive him to that awful death?

The picture is horrible. That of the blasted eyes is revolting. True, and for this reason it may not come within the artistic, as outlined in the philosophy of Longinus; but it is not my purpose here to be artistic. My very purpose is to visualize the horrible, because the only way for the people of this country to prevent this oncoming horror is to make the necessary military preparations for national defense.

But, young lady, this is not the end of the dreadful picture: Let us look into your home. The awful news comes—our men are beaten with enormous slaughter; father, brother, sweetheart —all your home's defenders—are dead. The invaders who have murdered them are in the street outside. There comes a summons at the door. A certain number of the enemy have been billeted to your house, and you must play the genial hostess. Though they get drunk, and ill-treat you beyond the power of words to tell, there remains no remedy. Your dear ones, who were your natural defenders, have been sacrificed on the altar of false faith in defenselessness as a deterrent of war.

CHAPTER V

THE NEEDS OF OUR ARMY

LETTER FROM GENERAL LEONARD WOOD

GOVERNOR'S ISLAND, N. Y.,
February 6th, 1915.

Dear Mr. Maxim:

I am very glad indeed to learn of your interest in military preparedness. The subject is one which is of vital importance to the American people. We do not want to establish militarism in this country in the sense of creating a privileged military class, dominating the civil element, receiving especial recognition, and exercising perhaps an undue influence upon the administration of national affairs, but we do want to build up in every boy a realization of the fact that he is an integral part of the nation, and that he has a military as well as a civic responsibility. All this can be done without creating a spirit of militarism or of aggressiveness. Take Switzerland as an example. Here we have a country where every boy and young man who is physically sound receives, largely as a part of his school work, military training to the extent necessary to make him an efficient soldier. This is a policy which ought to *be followed with our youth. It is not enough that a man should be willing to be a soldier. He should also be so prepared as to be an efficient one. This can only be accomplished through training. Switzerland and Australia have shown that this can be done through the public-school system, and with a resulting vast improvement in public morals and the quality of citizenship. The criminal rate in Switzerland is only a small fraction of ours. Respect for the law and constituted authorities, the flag of the country, and a high sense of patriotism are evident on all sides, and yet there is practically no standing army.*

We have here a patriotic people, living not with arms in their hands, or with a large standing army, but trained, equipped, and ready to efficiently and promptly defend the rights of their country. This I believe is the ideal we should strive for. We need a standing army big enough for the peace work of the day, i.e., the garrisoning of our foreign possessions, the Philippines, the Hawaiian Islands, Panama, the little garrisons in Porto Rico and Alaska, and a force in the continental United States adequate for the peace needs of the nation.

We must never again trust ourselves to the emergencies of a great war without proper preparation. If we do we shall meet with an overwhelming disaster. Preparedness is really an insurance for peace, and not an influence for war.

Photo of Painting by Sargent

Leonard Wood
Major General U.S. Army

To send our men untrained into war to meet equally good men, well trained and disciplined, was once described by Light Horse Harry Lee, of Revolutionary fame, as murder. Perhaps this is too strong, but it certainly is a gross disregard of human life.

Very truly yours,

LEONARD WOOD.

MR. HUDSON MAXIM,
    698 St. Mark's Ave.,
      Brooklyn, N. Y.

The facts given in this chapter have been gathered from many authoritative sources. It would be very comforting if these facts were known only to the American people, but unfortunately they are already known to the military authorities of all the other nations. Other nations are all very well aware of our unpreparedness; therefore, I am giving out no national secrets. English, German, French, Russian, and Japanese navy and military experts know exactly the men and equipment we possess.

It is the American people only who are not aware of the truth about our unpreparedness. This ignorance is largely due to the beguilers who have set the face of a great mass of our people against armaments, and have made them turn deaf ears to every voice that tries to rouse them to their danger.

Our ship of state has been drifting down stream like a raft. The only reason the raft has not been wrecked lies in the fact that we have been fortunate enough to have a pretty clear stream to ourselves all the while, with no breakers and no cataracts in sight. But there are breakers and rapids and cataracts down stream, and we are at last nearing them rapidly.

Even as long ago as 1880, General Emory Upton spoke thus prophetically:

"In time of war the civilian as much as the soldier is responsible for defeat and disaster. Battles are not lost alone on the field; they may be lost beneath the Dome of the Capitol, they may be lost in the Cabinet, or they may be lost in the private office of the Secretary of War. Wherever they may be lost, it is the people who suffer and the soldiers who die, with the knowledge and the conviction that our military policy is a crime against life, a crime against property, and a crime against liberty. The author has availed himself of his privilege as a citizen to expose to our people a system which, if not abandoned, may sooner or later prove fatal. The time when some one should do this has arrived."

In 1912, Admiral Kane said: "They told me in London, 'You are living in a fool's paradise.

Some day you will wake up with a fight on your hands, and you won't be ready for it.' "

Not only must the United States solve the great problem of shaping a military policy that will enable us to establish an adequate force for national defense in time of war, to build up and man our Navy, construct and man coast fortifications, and enlist, arm, and train an adequate army, but also there must be faced the far more difficult problem of enlisting the co-operation of the American people in the enterprise.

The fathers of our country, believing that a large standing Army would be a menace to the liberties of the people, ordained that our Army, in time of peace, should not exceed twenty-five thousand. Since then, Congress has several times raised the limit until we now may have an Army, in time of peace, of not more than a hundred thousand men. As a matter of fact, we have a regular Army of 93,016, both staff and line.

As this Army has to be spread out over our entire continental and outlying possessions, the sight of an American soldier of our regular Army is about as rare an occurrence as the sight of a sea-serpent.

Within the actual limits of our forty-eight states we have but 48,428 regular troops. Of these 17,947 must be kept in our coast fortifications, even as a pretense of garrisoning them. This leaves only 30,481 mobile troops, including engineers, cavalry, infantry, and field artillery. We have a militia on paper numbering 127,000, men and officers. Only 60,000 of these, however, are in readiness for service.

Therefore, we have in the United States to-day a regular Army of 48,000, and 60,000 militia ready for duty, or 108,000 men and officers altogether. In time of war not a man of our militia could well be spared for military service to repel an invader, for in such troublesome times they would all be needed for police duty to maintain order and obedience throughout the country.

General Wood recently told us that it would take a month to mobilize even our little Army of thirty thousand men.

Out of the 127,000 officers and men of the militia which we have on paper, only 60,000 being available, and only 30,000 of our regulars being available, we could place on the firing-line only 90,000 men and officers, and there would be no reserves.

When Napoleon, the world's greatest military captain, went into battle, he always kept a large and powerful force in reserve, to give confidence to those on the firing-line, and to save the day in case of a reverse, and possibly to turn defeat into victory, and at the worst to cover a retreat, and save the army from rout. This same need exists with us for a large national reserve of well-armed and well-trained men, ready to be called from

Number of Officers and Enlisted Men of United States Regular Army

Number Authorized, 100,000

Actual Number, 93,016

Total Number Mobile, 54,082

Total Number Mobile in Continental United States, 32,340

civil life to refill the depleted ranks of an army at the front.

Our regular Army is, in men and guns, but a mere nucleus of what we ought to have, and of what we must have to save this country from defeat and abject humiliation should war come.

Not only this—the artillery we have is without adequate field organization. It would take at least four months to train additional personnel in order to get our field artillery ready for duty. It would take us four times as long, therefore, to get our own artillery on the firing-line, ready for battle, on either our eastern or western seaboard, as it would for an enemy to get its artillery there.

It is we ourselves who are handicapped by isolation, not the enemy—isolation not of space, but of time.

If it be true that God fights on the side that is the best equipped with artillery, God could not be expected to fight on the side of our militia.

Our militia at the present time has only sixty-five organized batteries, with four guns each. It is absolutely imperative that we should have seventy-nine additional batteries, with six guns each, even moderately to complete our equipment in field artillery. Think of it! Our militia has less than half the number of field batteries necessary for battle.

It is also worthy of mention that these batteries are without ammunition trains, and without officers or men for the new organization, and we have not the necessary horses to draw the batteries we already have.

Our militia is entirely without siege artillery, while neither our militia nor our regular Army is equipped with field mortars or howitzers of the larger calibers now used abroad, which have been so terribly effective in the present war.

Not only are foreign nations far ahead of us in actual existing war strength in men and guns, but also they have each an efficient system whereby their present equipment may be rapidly expanded. We have no such system.

Our Fatal Isolation

Never yet have we perceived the important truth that in this age of war machinery, requiring months and years to create, isolation by time is an equivalent to isolation by distance. Our own isolation in the matter of the time required for us to raise and train armies and equip them with shoulder-rifles, automatic guns, quick-firing cannon, siege howitzers, ammunition supply trains, and to build, man, and equip with guns, battleships, battle-cruisers, torpedo-boat destroyers, submarines, and, no less important, to equip flying machines with trained aviators, would be a far more serious handicap to us than our isolation by the seas would be to our enemies.

The *Scientific American,* February 6, 1915, says:

"We could not supply the men for the necessary field-artillery organization for four months, or the ammunition trains and ammunition for a year and a half, and not a gun is yet made or appropriated for, for the volunteers. The militia is short in cavalry and requires over fifty additional troops of cavalry to provide the divisional cavalry alone. There is an alarming absence of auxiliary troops. Most of the militia cavalry is poorly mounted, much of it practically without mounts, and, with the exception of a few special organizations, has had little or no field training. It needs months of hard work in camp. Engineers, signal and medical troops of the militia are as a rule insufficient in number, deficient in organization, equipment, and reserve supplies, and very many of them are far below their prescribed strength and without available personnel to fill them up."

The following is quoted from a statement made before a Congressional committee in 1912, by General William Crozier, Chief of Ordnance of the United States Army, and one of the ablest officers that the Army has ever had:

"So far as transporting troops is concerned, the sea as a highway is not an obstacle, but a

facility. It is very much easier to get any number of troops across the Atlantic Ocean than it would be to get the same number over anything like the same distance on land. Marine transportation is the very best kind you can have; the easiest, least expensive, and most expeditious, if you are considering large bodies of troops and large amounts of material. The fuel charge for transportation in good tramp steamers does not amount to one two-hundred-and-fiftieth part of a cent per ton per mile. The sea is a splendid means of transportation. The distance is only ten days for a vessel of very moderate speed, and you can carry a thousand men on a vessel of 3,000 tons' capacity without any trouble at all. There are any number of vessels to be had, and there is no resistance on this side against a well-equipped force of a hundred thousand men."

SHORTAGE OF OFFICERS

We have in our regular Army to-day about 4,572 officers. The number of English officers killed, wounded, and missing during the first six months of the European war was, in round numbers, 5,000, a little more than the total number of our officers.

It has been estimated by the most able authorities, among them the editor of the *Scientific American*, whom I quote, that: " In case of invasion we would need 380,000 stationary volunteer coast-guard troops to guard the approaches to our cities and coast-defense works.'' We should also require an additional 500,000 men at the very least. To be rational, we should have a mobile army of a million men. In this enormous country a standing army of a million men would, comparatively speaking, be small. It would still be one-fifth the size of the German army, one-tenth the size of the Russian army, and it would be less than the available Japanese army. Surely this great Republic can afford to maintain a standing army equal to that of Japan!

The number of officers we have at the present time would, of course, be practically lost in our proposed mobile army of a million men. Radical and immediate measures should at once be taken to increase tenfold the officer-making capacity of West Point. Also, any private in the ranks should, by meritorious conduct manifesting military promise, be open to promotion to West Point, to complete his education there. This would be a tremendous stimulus and encouragement to the rank and file.

The burglar who has begun to plan to rob a house and has commenced inspection of the locality to keep tab on the movement of the police in the vicinity, has already declared war on that house. The bank-raider who has begun to spy on the cashier of a bank and the nocturnal habits of the people of the town, and has equipped himself with the kit of tools and the explosives to breach the vault where the cash lies, has already declared war on that bank.

In this same sense, and to this same extent, there is more than one nation that has already declared war on the United States. Their spies have been working among us for years, and they have the kit of tools and the explosives all ready to breach our Navy and our coast fortifications.

Our lack of field-guns for our artillery and our lack of ammunition are very clearly put in the *Scientific American* of February 13, 1915:

"We have in the hands of troops, or stored, 634 completed guns. We have under manufacture or contract, 226. These guns will probably not be completed for at least a year and a half. In other words, the number of completed guns is a little less than half the total number deemed necessary for the field force of 500,000 men, and provides no guns whatever for the coastguard troops or new volunteer organizations which will be required in addition to the 500,000 field force. Of ammunition, we have, made and under contract, approximately 30 per cent. for the entire project of guns (1,292). Half of this is under manufacture or contract, so that there is not more than 15 per cent. actually completed. For the guns on hand and under manufacture we have, of ammunition

[124]

Strength of Regular Armies on Peace Footing

Russia, 1,200,000
Germany, 830,000
France, 750,000
Austria-Hungary, 424,000
Italy, 300,000
Great Britain, 250,000
Japan, 225,000
United States, 93,016

on hand and under manufacture, about 41 per cent.; actually on hand, approximately, 20.5 per cent. For the guns actually made (634) we have 27 per cent. of the ammunition necessary. For the guns now in the hands of the regular army and militia we have about 44 per cent. of the ammunition necessary. It should be remembered, however, that the guns in the hands of the regular army and militia at the present time are less than half the guns required for these forces when properly equipped with guns, even under our scheme for the assignment of guns and ammunition, which is in both instances far lower than in any of the great armies today, and the present war has indicated, in the case of one great power at least, that the consumption of ammunition has exceeded twice their maximum estimates, and that the proportion of artillery will, in future, be increased.

"At the rate of even last year's appropriations, which were the largest made for field-artillery guns and ammunition, it will take between eight and nine years to complete our present modest estimate for guns and ammunition, and the necessary equipment in the way of ammunition trains and other accessories."

We are told in the Report of the Chief of Ordnance, 1914, that no permanent ammunition trains have been provided.

The following figures give the personnel of our

regular Army, and of our militia. They are taken from the Report of Major-General Wotherspoon, Chief of Staff of the United States Army, for the period from April 22, 1914, to November 14, 1914:

Actual strength of the United States Army, exclusive of Philippine scouts:

Officers 4,572
Men 88,444
Authorized strength:
Officers 4,726
Men 95,977
Hence, shortage:
Officers 154
Men 7,533

Of total enlisted strength, 22.50 per cent., including recruits and recruiting parties, belong to the non-combatant and non-effective class, and are not with the colors; 19.45 per cent. are in that branch whose special function is coast-defense.

Mobile army (engineers, cavalry, field artillery, and infantry) is 58.05 per cent. of actual strength, and comprises:

Officers 2,738
Men 51,344

Omitting cooks, musicians, scouts, etc., mobile strength is:

Officers 2,738
Men 45,968

Mobile strength in continental United States:

Enlisted men 30,481

Ammunition:
  We need .... 11,790,850 artillery rounds.
  We have on hand
    and being manu-
    factured ...... 580,000 " "
  We need .... 646,000,000 rifle cartridges.
  We have on hand
    and being manu-
    factured ...... 241,000,000 " "
  We need a supply of $9\frac{1}{2}$, $12\frac{1}{2}$, and $16\frac{1}{2}$ howitzers.
  We have only thirty-two 6-inch howitzers and smaller pieces, none larger.

Militia:
  Total enlisted men, 119,087, of which only 52.56 per cent. have had any rifle practice, and only 33.43 per cent. have qualified as second-class marksmen or better.

From the Report of the Chief of Staff for the year ending June 30, 1914, we learn that out of our 120,000 militiamen, 23,000 failed to present themselves for the annual inspection; 31,000 absented themselves from the annual encampment; and 44,000 never appeared on the rifle range from one year's end to the other.

Congressman Gardner tells us, further, that 60 per cent. of our militia were unable, in 1913, to qualify even as third-class marksmen, and that half of that 60 per cent. (30 per cent.) did not even try to qualify.

For years prior to the breaking out of the great European conflict, Lord Roberts pleaded with the English people, and prayed that they might hear his appeal to prepare for war with Germany. Like a voice crying in the wilderness, he called the British nation to arms. His voice was not heeded, and the nation did not arm.

The voice of Lord Roberts sounded harshly on the ears of sensitive English officialdom. Lord Haldane, to emphasize his attitude, disbanded 80,000 British troops at the very moment when England should have enlisted and begun to train 800,000. Also, he threatened to abolish Lord Roberts' pension if he did not keep quiet. The grand old soldier was spared by a kind Providence to stand on the firing-line when the great war came which he had foreseen, and there he saw thousands of his country's dead who had fallen from failure to regard his timely warning.

We have a Lord Roberts, too. There is a grand old American soldier who for years has appealed to us to fly to arms with all speed in preparation against war. He has even greater reason than Lord Roberts had, because our danger is many times greater than was England's danger. We are practically defenseless, while England was not.

I quote the following from the American Lord Roberts, General Leonard Wood:

". . . We have neither guns nor ammunition sufficient to give any general commanding an army in the field any assurance of success if attacked by an army of equal size which is supplied with its proper quota of field-artillery.

"The fire of modern field-artillery is so deadly that troops cannot advance over terrain swept by these guns without prohibitive losses. It is therefore necessary to neutralize the fire of hostile guns before our troops can advance, and the only way to neutralize the fire of this hostile field-artillery is by field-artillery guns, for troops armed with the small arms are as effectual against this fire until they arrive at about 2,000 yards from it as though they were armed with knives. This field-artillery material and ammunition cannot be quickly obtained. In fact, the Chief of Ordnance

*estimates that almost one year would be required
to supply the field-artillery guns needed with one
field army of a little less than 70,000 men. No war
within the past 45 years has lasted for one year,
so that after war is declared it would probably be
over before we could manufacture an appreciable
number of guns; and the same applies to ammunition.*

*"The Ordnance Department states that by run-
ning night and day with three shifts Frankford
Arsenal could turn out about 1,600 rounds of ammunition per day, and that if private manufacturers were given orders to run under war conditions they could begin deliveries of ammunition in
from three to four months, and after getting
under way could turn out about 100,000 or
200,000 rounds per month for two or three months,
and after a total time of six months the production would perhaps equal 250,000 rounds per
month. The best estimates indicate that at the
end of the first six months not to exceed 350,000
rounds could be procured from all sources, including the Government plant. After this six months
there would be no particular difficulty in securing
ammunition as rapidly as might be needed.*

*". . . It is my belief that . . . unless private
manufacturers are now encouraged to manufacture ammunition for our guns after war is declared, they will not be in any condition to do so*

until after the war is finished, and the supply of ammunition during the war will be limited to what the arsenals can turn out. At present this is about 1,600 rounds per day, running three shifts, and this ammunition, under ordinary battle conditions, could be fired by eight guns in one day of battle. If guns are not supplied on the battlefield with the ammunition which they can be reasonably expected to use, they are not efficient, and when a gun has exhausted the ammunition supplied it becomes as perfectly useless as junk; in fact, it is worse than junk, for it must be protected by other troops.

"In the Russo-Japanese War the Russians expended during the war, exclusive of the action around Port Arthur, 954,000 rounds.

"At Mukden in nine days they expended 250,000 rounds.

"One battery of eight guns at Mukden fired 11,159 rounds, or 1,395 rounds per gun.

"At Liaoyang eight Russian guns fired in three hours 2,500 rounds, or 312 per gun.

"During August 30 and 31 the First and Third Siberians, with 16 batteries of 8 guns each, fired 108,000 rounds, or 844 rounds per gun.

"At Schaho, in a four-days' fight, the artillery of the First Infantry Division—48 guns—fired 602 rounds per gun.

"At this same battle in 45 minutes, 20 minutes of which were not occupied by firing, 42 guns fired

8,000 rounds, or 190 rounds per gun in 25 minutes of actual firing.

"The War Department believes, after extended study, that in case of war with a first-class power an army of 500,000 men will be needed to give this country any chance of success against invasion, and that this force will be needed at once. To make it efficient it must be given its proper quota of field-artillery. To do this this artillery must be on hand, for it cannot be supplied after war is started. A municipality might as well talk about buying its fire-hose after the conflagration has started. A fire department without its proper equipment is worthless, irrespective of the number of men it has; and so would be your armies, unless you provide in peace the material which will make them effective in war."—Statement of facts by Major-General Leonard Wood, Hearings on Fortifications Bill, Dec. 9, 1913.

Is Congress to Blame?

The blame for our undefended condition is generally attributed to Congress. It is true enough that the main blame rests with Congress, but it must be remembered also that Congress represents the will of the people.

Every Congressman goes to Washington in the interest of his constituents. He goes there to dicker for them and to swap votes with other Congressmen in exchanging Congressional concession for Congressional concession. His constituents want a post-office in their district, or a river deepened, or widened, or want a navy yard in their state, and he is ready to vote for similar concessions to all other Congressmen who will vote for the concessions his constituents require. Every Congressman is mindful of the fact, and every time he returns home he is reminded of the fact that he has not been sent to Congress for his health, but for the health of his constituents, and if he hopes to be returned, he must see to it that he gets what they have sent him after.

They have not sent him there to support an appropriation bill for a larger army or a larger navy. The people are imbued with the belief that the country as a whole is big enough and prosperous enough to be safe. They know little or nothing, and care less, about national defenses. No calamity has ever come upon us for lack of defenses. Why should they worry? Also, they have been assured from the pulpit and the Chautauqua and by circulars sent out by the peace societies that we not only do not need more defenses, but, on the contrary, we do not need those we have; and they are asked to write personal letters to their Congressmen urging them to vote against any appropriations to increase our national defenses.

I am not arguing for a large standing army,

but merely for an adequate army—an army big enough to intercept an invading army that might be landed on our shores in the event of our Navy being destroyed or evaded.

The American people are imbued with the idea that a large standing army is a menace to liberty. Whatever justification there may be for this attitude, it is certain that, if we are to yield to this point of view, and get along with a comparatively small effective army, it is absolutely indispensable that we should have a navy certainly as powerful as any in the world, with the single possible exception of that of England. All arguments that may be made against a large standing army become arguments in favor of a very large navy.

In view of the comparative weakness of our present Navy, we need an effective army of at least a million men. If, however, our Navy were to be brought to first rank and the Swiss system of military training in public schools were to be adopted, we could get along with a much smaller army. By the adoption of such a system, we should soon have a very large trained reserve force in civil life, which could be drawn upon in case of need. Assuming the adequacy of our Navy and coast fortifications, General Wood believes that, if the Swiss system of military training in public schools were to be adopted, we could get along very well with a standing army of from 200,000 to 225,000 men.

A navy, however large, could not, by any possible stretch of the imagination, be termed a menace to our liberties, and, as ex-Secretary Meyer has said, we are rich enough to match dollars for national defense with any other nation in the world.

It is common belief that military training and service in preparation for national defense menace democratic institutions.

In the days of her greatest virility and military prowess, Rome was a republic. But we must not conclude, because a country is governed by a congress and a president elected by the people, that all its institutions are more free or less autocratic than the institutions of a limited monarchy, or even an absolute monarchy.

We, in the United States, often pass laws that are so arbitrary, unprecedented, unwarranted, and confiscatory, as to make absolutism wince. The cities of Germany are governed so wisely and so well that could we have that system transplanted here, it would be almost worth our while to invite German conquest of the country.

No man's patriotism rises higher than his realization of the need that his country has for him. None of us likes our taxes any too well. Nevertheless, they bring home to us a better realization of the interdependence of the government and the individual.

We love those for whom we make sacrifices, and those to whom we give favors. Benjamin Franklin, desiring the favorable regard of a prominent person, made it opportune for that eminent person to do Franklin a favor.

Conscription, like that enforced in Germany, makes good citizens. It implants in them a sense of duty and obligation to the government, and creates a greater respect for ruling power and for law and order.

In this country, the ideas of the average individual concerning his obligations to the government and the government's obligations to him are vague and crude to the last degree. Conscription would largely remedy this by teaching duty to the government.

The government has exactly the same right to levy on the individual for military service as it has to tax him for anything else. Just as the government has the right to tax the individual for financial support of the government, so it has the right to tax the individual for military support of the government. Conscription makes the government and the individual partners for the common welfare. Few persons in this country consider themselves partners of the government.

In ancient Sparta, all individuals were the property of the government; all children were owned by the state. Consequently, the people owned the state, and the state owned the people. It is proper that the state and the individual should own each other, insomuch as their interests are mutual, just the same as husband and wife own each other.

Perhaps the best system of preparing the youth and young men of a country for military service is that practised in Switzerland. Switzerland is a typical democracy, and yet no country in the world has a more universal and efficient system of military training for its youth and young men.

After the conclusion of the war of 1870, Germany, guided by the iron will of Bismarck, divulged to Switzerland that the mailed fist had an itching palm for Swiss territory. Immediately an army of a hundred thousand Swiss mobilized on the frontier. They were the best-armed, the best-trained, and altogether the most efficient soldiers in Europe. Every man of them could shoot to kill. They were the flower of the mountains. Bismarck concluded that the game was not worth the candle. If Switzerland had not been armed to the teeth and ready, that country to-day would be a part of Germany.

The Swiss have not the remotest idea of making an aggressive move on any neighboring country, but they hold themselves in perfect readiness to see to it that no other nation can find it profitable to make an aggressive move on Switzerland.

Switzerland makes her military training a part of her school system. The chubby, rosy-cheeked little Swiss boys are taught to play soldier with wooden imitation guns, and as they grow, the training later becomes more comprehensive, more exacting, more scientific, until, finally, the young men find real guns in their hands, find themselves commanded by, and receiving instructions from, real officers, and they are taught to shoot. When their school training is over, their military training and term of military service also are over. They are ready for civil life, but, too, they are ready at any moment for the call of their country from civil life to shoulder rifle and knapsack and go to the front.

This is the system that we should adopt in our country. It places no burden upon the schoolboy or the young man; on the contrary, it is a source of keen enjoyment, like any other manly game. The beneficial psychological effect is simple: The youth is taught obedience, his powers of perception are quickened, his alertness increased, his physique greatly strengthened, his health benefited, and his personal habits governed by laws of temperance and hygiene, with the result that his efficiency for usefulness in all the business and affairs of civil life afterward is greatly enhanced. Thus, in Switzerland, the earning power of the population is increased out of all proportion to the cost for the training and maintenance of the entire army.

Mr. Richard Stockton, Jr., in his book, "Peace Insurance," ably expresses the value of military training, as follows:

"Military training has an important value entirely apart from its actual military value. This is conclusively proven in the numerous military schools of the United States. The majority of these schools disclaim any attempt to train soldiers, but include military training merely to make better citizens. They find that the man trained militarily learns obedience, promptness, cleanliness, orderliness, coolness, and secures that priceless asset known as executive ability—the ability to make others obey. Such schools form a stronger character and make better men.

"If this is true in a military school, it must be equally so with similar training received elsewhere. If thousands of parents pay from $500 to $1,500 per year to secure this training for their boys, surely there is some gain to the nation in the men who receive this training in the army. The fact is too well attested by educators throughout the world to admit of serious questioning."

It is possible that German militarism, by becoming absolutism, has grown from servant to master in Germany. However this may be, one thing is certain, that German progress in the industrial arts and sciences, in municipal and general government economics, has made the German people more efficient and potential per capita than the people of any other country on earth. Consequently, we must admit either that the Germans are inherently superior intellectually to the people of other nations, or that they have acquired their present economic superiority by reason of some procedure which they have followed, and with which other nations have not kept pace.

The natural assumption is that militarism is responsible for the German culture of efficiency. It is not an unreasonable conclusion, in view of the evidence, that German militarism is the greatest school of economics that the world has ever seen.

CHAPTER VI

THE NEEDS OF OUR NAVY

"Look at the accomplished rise of Japan; think of the possible national awakening of China; and then judge of the vast problems of the Pacific. Only those Powers who have great navies will be listened to with respect when the future of the Pacific comes to be solved."

Kaiser Wilhelm II.

A FAMOUS English philosopher once took his son to the House of Parliament, and said to him, "Now, my boy, I want you to witness with what ignorance and irrationality we are governed."

Were that same philosopher and his son to witness some of our American legislative proceedings, he would find still greater ignorance and inconsistency for the edification of his son.

The fathers of our country thought it necessary to the security of our government that all naval and military authority should be subordinate to the civil authority. Congress is able absolutely to dominate the Army and Navy. The Secretary of War and the Secretary of the Navy are generally civilian politicians. It certainly does seem inconsistent to take a man out of civil life, who, very likely, may be wholly ignorant of naval and

military matters, and, through preconceived prejudice, unalterably opposed to actual naval and
military needs, and place him in a position seri-
ously to interfere with the work of the officers
who have been educated at government expense
at West Point and Annapolis.

The Secretary of the Army and the Secretary
of the Navy ought not to be changed, regardless
of merit, or the lack of it, every time we change
a President. Those important offices should be
lifted out of politics. A man's political qualifications for an office usually depend not a whit upon
his being suited to the office by his ability to perform the duties of the office, but simply upon what
he has done for the party to earn the appointment.

There is a huge difference between political
merit and official merit. Political merit relates
entirely to party service, and may constitute de-
merit when squared with the generally accepted
moral code and standard of human behavior. A
Secretary of the Army or a Secretary of the Navy
may, by previous training, ignorance, effeminacy,
or, even worse, by pacific bias, be entirely un-
suited to such a position and entirely incapable of
broadly perceiving militant duty.

Such changing of our war and naval secretaries
is as harmful as it would be to change the head
of a hospital every month, with the same disregard of qualifications derived from previous edu-

cation, training, and experience. Evidently, it would be disastrous to place in supreme command of a hospital first an allopath, then change him a month later for a homeopath, replace the homeopath with an osteopath, followed by a Christian Science healer, then a spiritualistic clairvoyant, finally a Hindoo swami. Such a rotation of hospital heads would hit the patients pretty hard.

When, however, we get a Secretary of the Navy of the caliber of Theodore Roosevelt, or of ex-Secretary Meyer, then the Navy profits by having a civilian for its head, because such men as these, who are natural judges and masters of men, are able to make use of the greater knowledge and experience of those under them, and they have the additional advantage of being *en rapport* with the civilian's point of view, while from the fact that they are civilians, they escape the unreasoning prejudice of the anti-militarists, who believe that all naval and military men are actuated by ulterior motives and self-interest when trying to get Congressional support for the Army and Navy.

A man who, through study and experience, has become a specialist in a certain line of work, is better qualified to do work in that line and to know its needs than is a person who has had no such knowledge and no such experience. In legal matters, we go to a lawyer to get advice, and we generally take it, and pay for it. There is an old saw that he who acts as his own lawyer has a fool for a client.

The American Congress is composed almost entirely of civilians, who are qualified neither by study nor experience to pass judgment on the needs of our Army and Navy. They are as unable correctly to diagnose the condition of our Navy and to prescribe rational remedies as a pastry cook would be to diagnose and operate for appendicitis, or to prescribe for the treatment of pneumonia.

It is hard to understand how there could be any one in the country unable to perceive this patent truth—that a person educated and trained to a thing all his life ought to know more about that thing than a person who has had no such training and no such experience.

Yet the officers of the Army and Navy are not permitted to give public expression to their views on naval and military needs.

I quote from the New York *Times* the following remarks on a significant incident:

"Washington, Feb. 17, 1915.—Secretary Garrison to-day instructed Brigadier-General Scott, chief of staff of the army, to call upon Captain William Mitchell, of the general staff, to explain published remarks attributed to him on the unpreparedness of the United States for war.

"Captain Mitchell was quoted as having said

that 'it would take the United States about three years to put an army of one million trained men in the field, and in that time an enemy could take and hold our American seaboards.'

"Secretary Garrison said he considered such utterances, if made in public at present, injudicious and improper."

When a hunter goes out with a gun after game, he does not consider it good sport to shoot a four-footed beast or flying fowl without first giving the victim a chance for its life, and an opportunity to give the alarm to its fellows; yet our army and navy men, under the present gag rule, are not given a sportsman's chance to escape being shot, through our national unpreparedness, or even to give a cry of warning to their fellows. Even the murderer is given a chance to present his case before being executed, but the American soldier is not afforded any such opportunity.

Our Congress allows itself to be dominated by impossible pacific ideas, and consequently neglects to take the necessary sane precautions to safeguard the country against war, or even to avert disaster in case of war, and yet, when there arises a *casus belli*, Congress feels no moral compunction against declaring war and sending its ill-equipped, thin-ranked, ill-provided Army to the front to face inescapable death.

If the troops run out of ammunition on the

firing-line, they cannot retire, but must keep their line unbroken, even though they are all killed.

At the battle of Spottsylvania Court House, in the Civil War, the regiment in which my brother Leander served was caught in exactly this position. They had been drawn up to defend a baggage train. They held their places, and loaded and fired until their ammunition was exhausted; and still they held their places under a rain of bullets from the enemy, until reënforcements came. Of that company, which went into the fight a hundred strong, eighty-four were killed, among them my brother.

In war, the lives of a few hundred, or even a few thousand soldiers, count for nothing, if the position they are holding has a greater strategic value than their lives. When food runs short, it sometimes becomes strategically a good bargain to sacrifice the lives of a thousand men in a forage raid to bring in a thousand sheep. In such a case, a sheep is worth more than a man, because the sheep can be eaten, and the man cannot.

There are some things in this world that we are able to know are absolutely wrong. Of these, nothing is surer than that it is wrong to forbid our army and navy officers the public expression of their opinions, which would give the country the benefit of their knowledge and experience. Not only this, but it is a great injustice to the officers of the Army and the Navy, for, if war comes, it is they who will have to stand on the firing-line—not the individuals of civilian officialdom.

When, in the near future, our fleet is sent to intercept the on-coming superior fleet of an enemy, those officers who must stand on the bridge and at their posts on the decks—and go down with their ships—are the very men now gagged by civilian red tape.

If they could speak, and tell you and me and all of us the truth and the naked truth, then very likely their lives could be saved, and the sacrifice of their ships and their crews avoided.

If the actual truth about our defenselessness were generally appreciated, our whole people, as Antony said of the stones of Rome, "would rise and mutiny" against the legislative and bureaucratic officialdom and the fanatical peace propaganda that are teaching the people ignorance and folly while muting the tongues of those who should speak.

A nation is but a composite individual. Just as the male head of the family, being the natural protector of the family, has, in all ages, needed strong arms for the defense of the family, so, in all ages, have nations needed strong arms for national defense. These are the army and the navy. When army and navy are weak, then the nation, regardless of other elements of prowess, is correspondingly weak, and, more than that, the nation that is not safeguarded by a strong army and a strong navy is a poor nation, regardless of its resources and visible wealth. For the value of wealth and resources is very largely dependent upon their security—upon the power of the army and navy to defend or guarantee the title to them.

That man is not a rich man, the title to whose property is questionable and likely at any time successfully to be disputed. The value of wealth depends entirely upon the ability of its possessor to control and utilize it, which includes the ability to defend his title to it.

The same thing holds true with a nation. The value of its wealth depends entirely upon its ability to control and utilize it, subject absolutely to ability to defend it.

You and I, reader, may count ourselves worth a certain sum. But if our property is not so safeguarded as to ensure our continued possession and benefit of it, and to ensure to our children and our children's children the possession and benefit of it, then we are by no means so rich as we should be were our title guaranteed by adequate national defenses.

We are at once the richest country in the world, and, in proportion to our wealth, the poorest; for, in proportion to our wealth, we are the most defenseless. By consequence, we are without guaranty of title to our property, and we may at any time be robbed of it.

An adequate army and an adequate navy are the only possible means by which American titles to property can be guaranteed.

Just as it is worth all it costs, and more, for owners of real estate to have the title to their property guaranteed by a title-guarantee company, and just as the property is by such guaranty enhanced in value more than the cost of the guaranty, so the guaranty of title to American property dependent upon an adequate army and navy is worth far more than the entire cost of them, by virtue of enhanced values.

When a nation, like the United States, has become a World Power, with outlying possessions in distant seas and within the spheres of influence of other powerful nations, it assumes obligations just in proportion to the hazards involved in the maintenance of title. Also, when a nation, like the United States, has a world-compassing commerce, its obligations are just as large as its commerce, and its need of a navy adequate to defend its commerce is, for that purpose alone, exactly as great as its need of the commerce. But, in addition to this great need, there is the still greater need of a navy of such magnitude and potentiality as effectually to safeguard the country against invasion.

Although we should have an army of sufficient size and possessed of so efficient equipment as ultimately to repel invasion, still the cost in life and treasure for repulsion and expulsion would exceed many times the cost of the warships and naval equipment necessary to prevent invasion.

The American people are not all agreed that we should have a navy. There is a very large percentage of the population who believe that we ought not to have any at all. But there is one ground, I think, for common agreement: Admiral Austin M. Knight, President of the Naval War College, one of the best-informed and ablest officers in the Navy, as well as one of the most scholarly men in the country, says:

"If we are to have a navy it should be as efficient as it can possibly be made. And everybody who knows anything about the Navy knows that this is not its present condition."

I shall quote further from a recent speech of Admiral Knight:

"There is much about the Navy which is splendidly efficient. But as a whole it is far less efficient than it can and ought to be. Our ships are fine. Our officers are capable, industrious, and ambitious. Our enlisted men are the equals of those in other navies. But efficient ships and officers and men do not alone make an efficient navy. They must be welded into an efficient whole by a unity of organization and administration

Photo by Ernst

Austin M. Knight

and purpose which coördinates their capabilities and directs their efforts towards a common end, wisely selected and very clearly seen. Here is the first point at which we are lacking. We are lacking also in that harmonious composition of the fleet which is needed to give to every element of it the support that it needs from other elements, to make up a symmetrical and well-balanced whole. And we are lacking to a marked degree in absolutely essential facilities for the care and preservation of our ships, especially in the matter of dry-docks.

"Finally, we are lacking in efficient organization of the personnel. Here, so far as officers are concerned, the conditions are altogether deplorable. In a service like the Navy, where spirit is everything, where enthusiasm must be the driving power back of every activity, I ask you to picture the effect of a condition where a young officer, graduating from the Naval Academy full of spirit and enthusiasm, finds himself confronted with a prospect of promotion to the grade of Lieutenant at the age of 52 years.

"If you ask me who is responsible for these conditions, I can only reply that the responsibility comes home to nearly all of us. Some of it, I am sure, rests with me;—much of it, I believe, with you. Certainly it cannot be attributed in excessive measure to any one administration of the Navy Department, for it has existed for half a *century at least. So let us not cloud the issue by assuming that it is a new condition, and that all administrations up to some recent date have been models of wisdom and efficiency, or that Naval Officers themselves have always been ready with good advice. Speaking as the representative of Naval Officers as a body, I frankly admit that we have not always seen clearly what was needed, and have not always worked together even for ends which we did see clearly. As for the Secretaries of the Navy, it is not surprising that many of them have failed to realize that their first duty was to strive, in season and out of season, to promote the War efficiency of the Navy as a whole. Many of them have not remained in office long enough to learn this. Some, perhaps, have realized it more or less clearly but have not found at hand an organization through which they could produce results. A few have made material contributions toward improved conditions. . . .*

"A large part of the responsibility, especially that connected with the small size and the unbalanced composition of the Fleet and the lack of dry-docks, rests with Congress, which has always approached naval legislation from the wrong side so far as efficiency is concerned;—asking, not what do we need for efficiency? but what can we afford to spend for efficiency? Behind the responsibility of Congress lies the responsibility of the Country,—and you, gentlemen, represent the

Country—because it has not insisted upon having what was needed, without reference to cost. It may be that this attitude of both Congress and the Country is necessary and even inevitable. But I am one of those who believe that this great Country of ours can afford to have anything in the way of national defense which it needs, and I assume that all present here to-night agree that we need a navy, and if a navy, then an efficient one, and that whatever efficiency costs is the measure of what we can afford to spend.

"What constitutes an adequate Navy for the United States? The answer will depend, of course, upon the purpose for which we assume that the Navy is to be used. We are all agreed, I presume, that it is not to be used for aggression. Is it, then, to be used solely for defense? If we answer 'yes,' we ought to do so with a full recognition of what we are to defend and also of the elementary maxim that the best defense is a vigorous offense. In other words, no matter how resolute we may be to use our Navy only for repelling aggression, it does not follow that we should plan for meeting the aggressor only at our gates. Even if we had no interests outside our borders and no responsibilities for the defense of our outlying possessions and dependencies, we should still, as reasonable beings not wholly ignorant of history, prepare to project our battle line toward the enemy's coasts and to assume a

*course which would throw upon him the burden
of replying to our initiative. In this sense, then,
we need a navy for offense; that is to say, for offensive action with a defensive purpose. In shaping our plans along these lines, we should not
overlook the fact that the policy which dictates
the measure of our defense must take full note of
the larger national policy which it is to enforce;—
in relation, for example, to the Monroe Doctrine,
the Panama Canal, the Philippines, and other
matters which are at once of national and of international significance."*

If the United States does not need a navy, then
we should dispose of the fighting ships we have
and disband the personnel. If, on the other hand,
we do need a navy, there is one consideration,
and one consideration alone, that can rightfully
determine the size and power of that navy—
namely, its adequacy to serve the purpose for
which it is intended.

A fighting ship is built, equipped with armament, manned, and coaled for one sole purpose—
that of adequacy in a fight. Its success or failure
—in short, its usefulness or uselessness—depends
entirely upon its fighting adequacy against a possible opponent. An ocean-liner is built, manned,
and coaled to fight tempestuous seas, and safely
make the voyage; but unless the ship is built sufficiently staunch, has sufficiently powerful engines,

is well manned, and has coal enough for the trip, it is in no sense a success, or useful; on the contrary, it is an utter failure and worse than useless.

The same thing holds true of a navy: Unless it can defeat the fleet of an enemy, and return from the voyage, it is a failure, and worse than useless.

A naval disaster in our present condition would be likely to be an irreparable calamity, while a naval victory might likely win the war. It is for this big difference that we need a navy. Consequently, the entire use of a navy may be summed up in the one word, *superiority* over a possible enemy.

When two men run for a municipal office all the votes cast for the loser are of no value to the loser, and all campaign funds spent in getting them have been wasted; the only votes that are of value to the winner are those that constitute his majority. Similarly, in a naval battle, it is the majority of votes cast by the winning guns that secures the victory, for all of the other votes cast by the guns are balanced by an equal number of votes cast by the guns of the enemy.

The total value of a navy may be summed up in the value of one battleship, which gives a conquering preponderance in gun-fire.

Admiral Knight recently said:

"The War College considers that every effort of the Fleet, and every effort of the Department in connection with the Fleet, should have for its sole aim the war efficiency of the Fleet. Every effort which does not directly contribute to this end is in itself a wasteful expenditure of energy, and so far as it is a diversion from this end, is distinctly harmful."

Among all those who have occupied positions of trust and power, and whose business it has been to recognize and provide for our naval and military needs, it is remarkable how few have had the necessary breadth of view to grasp the strategic situation, and perceive its requirements without making silly and costly mistakes, like that of the construction of our first three battleships, the *Oregon,* the *Massachusetts,* and the *Indiana,* merely for coast-defense purposes. None of these ships was qualified for service in distant waters. Then, when the war with Spain came, we held our breath while the *Oregon* rounded the Horn. Think of the United States of America being in such straits for fighting ships as actually to hang national hope on the old *Oregon.* A single shell from one of the huge guns of an up-to-date British super-dreadnought has a striking force equal to the energy required to lift the old battleship *Oregon* bodily to a height of more than six feet. There is no middle course for the United States.

We must play the game as a World Power, and as other nations are playing the game. To get fair play we must provide ourselves with the weapons with which they are providing themselves. If we do not, we shall be brushed aside with a ruthless hand, and shall find our commerce circumscribed on every side by inimical spheres of influence— dead lines over which we shall not dare to pass.

It is necessary for us not only to fortify the Panama Canal, but also to maintain a navy of sufficient prowess to enable us to reach that Canal at all times, and under all conditions, for it is indispensable that we maintain communication with our defenses there.

Should we become involved in war with England or Germany, the navy of either being more powerful than ours, we should be immediately isolated from the Panama Canal zone. Similarly, Japan could successfully blockade the Pacific approaches to the Canal.

We have, at enormous expense, cut a great waterway through the Isthmus, and established a short route between the Atlantic and the Pacific. The Canal is our property. Other nations of the world may use it. We generously built it for the world's welfare. It will, however, be valuable in time of war for the passage of our warships; in fact, it will be a vital necessity to us. But our ability to use it for that purpose will be entirely dependent upon the ability of our Navy to keep the sea clear of an enemy's ships at either end.

The war with Spain was very useful, because it brought the truth home to us that the command of the American seas is absolutely vital to us. Immediately following the Spanish War, we rapidly built up our Navy, until it became second only to that of England. But we have, of late years, been slipping back, until now our Navy occupies third place, with a likelihood of soon dropping down to fifth place.

In 1905, England evolved the great modern dreadnought, which was as much of a revolution over existing types of fighting ships as was Ericsson's *Monitor* over the fighting ships of its time. The dreadnought relegated all existing battleships to the second line.

The dreadnought was so much superior in size, in speed, in gun-fire, and in all defensive and offensive qualities, that it took its place at once as the indispensable first-line battleship. England, Germany, France, Japan, each recognizing the tremendous superiority of the dreadnought, enlarged their naval appropriations, and built dreadnoughts.

The American Congress, however, failed to recognize the serious character of the crisis. It failed to appreciate the fact that the dreadnought meant a revolution in battleship construction. Instead of naval appropriations being increased according to our needs, they were decreased. As a result, there are now two nations at least that could whip us off the seas, while the navies both of France and Japan are likely very soon to rank above us.

All our illusions about our splendid isolation would vanish with the destruction of our fleet. A European Power could, in less than two weeks, land upon our shores an army of from 100,000 to 200,000 men. Here, the question naturally arises: How would they be able to get past our coast fortifications? We have spent about $160,000,000 on our coast fortifications, but they were never intended for the protection of our entire coast line. They were intended only to defend our important cities and harbors and naval bases. They actually protect but a very small fraction of our many thousand miles of shore.

As the *Scientific American* has justly stated, our coast fortifications should not be so named; instead, they should be designated as city-and-harbor fortifications.

It would be quite impracticable adequately to defend our long stretch of seaboard by means of coast fortifications. The only coast fortifications that can effectually serve us are battleships. It is absolutely indispensable to our integrity as a nation that we have a fleet sufficiently powerful to defend our whole coast against invasion.

These questions present themselves: How are we to ascertain what our naval needs are? How shall we prepare to meet them? Of whom shall we seek guidance?

Several years ago the Navy Department organized the General Board of the Navy, headed by Admiral Dewey. This Board studied our needs with great diligence and care, and Congress was advised accordingly.

All the leading navies of the world have a technical body corresponding to our General Board, but in other countries that body speaks with authority, while our General Board may only advise. Congress pays but little attention to these advisers. It is a principle of our government that the voice of the greatest number shall rule, and the people of this country have come to believe that the majority is more likely to be right than the minority. Many falsely believe that in the matter of wisdom there is safety in mere numbers; that the opinion of a hundred men is of more value than the opinion of a single man.

Multiplying the number of individuals possessing a limited amount of knowledge and an unlimited amount of ignorance does not raise the high-water mark of their united wisdom. Wisdom means intellectual height. Some men are seven feet high intellectually, while others are not more than a foot high.

The average of conscientiousness is much higher than the average of intelligence. A man's sincerity cannot be used as a yard-stick for measur-

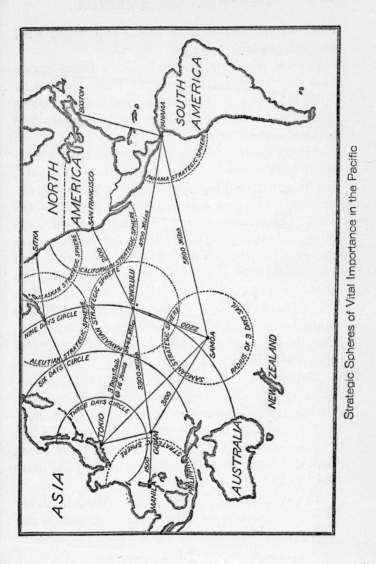

Strategic Spheres of Vital Importance in the Pacific

ing his intellectual height. Sincerity and conscientiousness are sister entities, and are largely a measure of intellectual bias, whose other name is prejudice.

We may compare the intellectual height of men with one another in a manner similar to comparing their physical height, only there is a much greater disparity in the intellectual than there is in the physical. If we take a man six feet high, and stand another man beside him of equal or less height, the height of the two men is no greater than that of the first man. If we add a hundred men of average height, we shall find that the average height of the whole line is considerably less than that of the six-footer with whom we started.

The same thing holds true with the intellectual height of men. We may put a man in each chair in the House of Representatives and in the Senate, and the total height of the voting wisdom of the majority will be only the average height of that majority, and it will be less than that of one man who might be selected for his wisdom from their number.

Any one member of the General Board of the United States Navy is likely to know much more about the needs of the Navy and what Congress should do for the Navy than is known by all members of the House and Senate put together.

Representative Gardner very possibly knows more about our naval and military needs and what Congress ought to do for the Army and Navy than is known by all the other members in Congress. In fact, he may likely know more about the subject and be able to advise the country with greater wisdom upon our needs for national defense than a line of average Congressmen standing shoulder to shoulder in a string that would girdle the earth.

Napoleon said, "He goes fast who goes alone." Always, the great national issues that make history have been decided in each case by one man, and all great national crises have depended upon the decisive action of one man. In recognition of this principle, Rome, in times of great peril, chose a dictator.

The Medo-Persian empire was the architecture of one man, Cyrus the Great. The Persian empire was conquered and destroyed by the genius of one man, Alexander the Great. Rome was brought to her knees by one man, Hannibal. He ultimately failed, and Carthage was destroyed, because of one man, an eloquent enemy of Hannibal, Hanno, at home in Carthage, who was a peace-advocate. Rome was saved from destruction at the hands of the Teutons and Cimbri solely by the military genius of Marius. Cæsar walked alone through Gaul, solitary in his height above his whole army; by comparison, all men of his age were pygmies. Charles Martel alone saved Europe from the

Moors. Peter the Great, the amazing architect of Russia, was impatient of advice and brooked no interference with his purpose. Cromwell alone was the governing brain of England. Frederick the Great was great because he played the game of war lone-handed. Napoleon Bonaparte was so intellectually tall that he towered over Europe like a colossus, and he played kings like pawns in the game of war. Bismarck played a lone hand in the creation of the German empire. During the entire Civil War, Abraham Lincoln parried with wit the advice of friends. To his enemies, he masked with mirth an inscrutable purpose, while he sat solemn and solitary at the helm.

So, always and always, it has been. Great national games have been games of solitaire.

We need a national leader who shall have such size and quality of brain, and be possessed of such soul, courage, and wisdom as shall qualify him to use the power of his high office to the full to help save this country from the dire calamity that is impending.

Although the General Board knows a thousand times more about our needs and what we ought to do to provide for them than is known to the entire American Congress, still Congress, dominated by the pride of ignorance, believes that it knows best, oblivious to the fact that the voiced ignorance of a thousand men may have less truth in it than the voiced wisdom of a single man.

Members of Congress assume the responsibility of deciding what the strength of the Navy shall be, and what shall be its composition. Congress, not the General Board, decides how many battleships, cruisers, destroyers, and submarines we shall have; how many officers and men they shall carry. The result is disastrous, for our Navy is inefficient and ill-balanced. It is dangerously weak where it should be strongest.

During the administration of Lord Haldane (then Mr. Haldane) the British Admiralty Board resigned because four battleships had been cut from the estimates for new construction, which were set at the minimum of national requirements; and it is due to forcing the matter by this action that the British have the four big battle-cruisers, of the *Queen Elizabeth* type, carrying 15-inch guns, which throw a shell weighing 1,925 pounds, and which out-range all other guns on ships.

Robert Blatchford, whom Mr. Winston Churchill dubbed a "ridiculous Jingo," said, in a remarkable series of articles written before the outbreak of the present war for *The Daily Mail* in the hope of arousing the British public to their danger:

"But the British people do not believe it. The British people take little interest in foreign affairs, and less in military matters. The British people do not want to bother, they do not want to pay, they do not want to fight, and they regard

as cranks or nuisances all who try to warn them of their danger.

"The danger is very great, and is very near. It is greater and nearer than it was when I began to give warning of it, more than five years ago. . . .

"The people are conceited, self-indulgent, decadent, and greedy. They want to keep the Empire without sacrifice or service. They will shout for the Empire, but they will not pay for the Empire or fight for it. Germany knows this. The world knows it. The Cabinet Ministers know it. But no Minister dares to say it. We are in sore need of a man. . . .

"While the articles have been appearing in The Daily Mail I have received letters of strong approval from Lord Roberts and Lord Charles Beresford, and from many officers of the Army and the Navy.

"Are all these men ignorant and stupid, and are political wisdom and military knowledge confined in these islands to the lawyer who runs our Army, the lawyer who runs our Navy, and the simpering nonentities who edit the Nonconformist organs?

"The Liberal Government made a fatal blunder when they hesitated to lay down the four extra dreadnoughts. They were trying to economize. They were hoping for a cheaper way out of the difficulty. They were waiting for something to *turn up. The Germans knew this, and made a tremendous effort to get ahead of us. It is not safe to trust the tradition of Micawber against the tradition of blood and iron.*

"Had the British Government, instead of trying to save a few millions, asked the nation boldly for the full amount required, and set about the necessary work in earnest, the Pan-Germans might have had an unpleasant time with the German taxpayer.

"It is time our Government and people recognized the facts. Germany has challenged us. If we show weakness we are lost. We cannot bluff our enemy. We cannot evade him. We cannot buy safety for an old song. We can only hold our own against so powerful and resolute an antagonist by showing an equal power and resolution.

"In the crisis to which I have just referred we took the weak course when we ought to have taken the strong one. Economy at such a time is the most profligate extravagance.

"When the Government held the four dreadnoughts back, they should have been pushing a dozen dreadnoughts forward; when they tried to save a few millions they should have laid out fifty millions. Instead of reducing the artillery and pottering about with a handful of Territorials they should have demanded an Army.

" But the Cabinet were afraid. We want a man. . . .

"I do not want war; I want peace. I am not an enemy of the Germans, but a friend. I like Germany; but I love England, as a man loves his mother, or his wife, or his comrade, or his home.

"And the Empire is in danger; and we are unready; and we need a man. . . .

"If only we can get the British people to understand in time."

Now, reader, carefully weigh this wonderfully prophetic language, spoken by an Englishman to the English people, before the great war came, which is now wringing millions upon millions of pounds sterling from the English purse, and wringing blood from the veins of thousands upon thousands of young men gathered from the length and breadth of the whole empire, and wringing tears from millions of mourning eyes; let us take this powerful appeal of Blatchford to the English people and conceive it to be my own appeal now, to you and the whole American people. We are in the same danger that England was, and unless we prepare as England did not prepare we shall be wrung even more than England is wrung.

Our naval officers, who, more than all others, know what we should have in kinds of ships, in numbers of ships, and in personnel, are ignored. It is a case of the blind leading those who see clearly.

After the most careful and thorough investigation and weighing of our Navy's actual needs, the General Board of the Navy figures closely, as near to the danger point as they dare, in order that their recommendations may stand a better chance of approval by Congress. But Congress assumes that, being naval men, they have an ax to grind and are naturally strongly biased in the direction of extravagance, and the Board's wise recommendations are accordingly discounted.

We have only 33 battleships less than twenty years old, eleven of which belong to the second line, with four building and authorized, which will make 37 in all. The General Board thinks that we should have 48 battleships less than twenty years old.

We have but 68 destroyers, while the General Board thinks that we should have 192 destroyers.

The General Board thinks that we could squeeze along with a minimum of 71,000 men to man our present fleet, without taking into account additional trained men needed for signal and tactical work on board auxiliary vessels, and without any provision for warships now building. As a bare fact, we have only 52,300 men. Thus we are short 18,000 of the men needed to man the fleet we have. In addition to this, there is a shortage in sight of 4,000 men required to man the fighting ships that will go into commission in 1915 and 1916.

Our naval experts tell Congress that we shall need 50,000 more men for the Navy as soon as they

Battle Ship Strength of the Nations

England—Dreadnoughts, 46   Battle Cruisers, 9

Germany—Dreadnoughts, 28   Battle Cruisers, 5

United States—Dreadnoughts, 15

France—Dreadnoughts, 12

Japan—Dreadnoughts, 10—Battle Cruisers, 2

Russia—Dreadnoughts, 11

Italy—Dreadnoughts, 10

can be enlisted and drilled; but the ears of Congress are deaf to the appeal. Yet a whisper for a new post-office can be heard by a Congressman from his home district a thousand miles away.

We have only 7,700 men in our naval militia. We have no naval reserve.

Congressman Gardner informs us, as a result of his investigations, that it would take five years to get a reserve of 25,000 sailors.

Our best-informed naval officers recommend for coast defense the immediate construction of a hundred submarines of the latest and most successful type. As a matter of fact, this number is far too few. We now have but 58 submarines, including those built, building, and authorized to be built. Many of those we have are obsolete and absolutely worthless.

The following is an extract from a report by the General Board of the Navy in 1913, which is very enlightening:

"The absence of any definite naval policy on our part, except in the General Board, and the failure of the people, Congress, and the executive government to recognize the necessity for such a policy, has already placed us in a position of inferiority which may lead to war; and this inferiority is progressive and will continue to increase until the necessity for a definite policy is recognized and that policy put into operation."

A fleet, to be effective, must be so constituted, organized, and trained as to benefit in the highest degree from team work. It must be able, like a baseball team, to act with the precision of a machine.

In addition to battleships, a fleet must have an appropriate number of battle-cruisers, smaller cruisers, transports, scouts, destroyers, submarines, colliers, tank-ships, supply ships, repair ships, mine-laying ships, tenders, and gunboats. Hospital ships should not be forgotten.

Admiral Fiske says:

"We have only one mine-layer. We need five additional mine-layers. On board that one mine-layer are only 336 mines. Germany had 20,000 mines when the war started."

A fleet without fuel-ships is like a fleet without stokers. A fleet without scouts is blind. It cannot see the enemy's movements, while its own movements lie under the eyes of the enemy. The videttes are called the eyes of an army. Similarly, the scouts of a fleet are the eyes of the fleet. A fleet without these eyes, when hunted by a fleet that has them, is in the same position as a hunted ostrich with its head hidden in the sand. Of these fast scouts, with minimum speed of 25-30 knots an hour, we have only three; Germany has 14, and Great Britain has 31.

Two fleets maneuvering for attack—one provided with scouts and the other without them—are relatively in the position of two men, armed with revolvers, fighting in a room, one blindfolded and the other with eyes uncovered.

As Admiral Knight has observed, battleships alone do not make a fleet, much less a navy. Our fleet is greatly weakened by our lack of destroyers. A fleet should always be accompanied by a large number of these vessels to support the scouts, and also to do scout duty themselves. They stiffen the screen about the battleships, and, when an opening is present, they are ready to dash against the enemy.

In the Civil War and in the Spanish War we were able largely to employ improvised merchant vessels for fuel-ships and scouts; for the sole reason that our enemies were even more miserably unprepared than ourselves. Had we, at the time of the Spanish War, been called upon to fight a really first-class Power, we should have been swept off the seas.

Fuel-ships and scouts cannot be improvised under modern conditions. They must be ready before war comes. It is just as fallacious to imagine that we can strengthen our Navy with improvised ships and personnel after war is declared, and get it in trim to meet a modern fleet in the pink of condition of preparedness, as it would be for an invalid cripple to imagine that he could train and get into condition for a victorious fight with a John L. Sullivan after entering the ring.

Of all arts and sciences, that of war is the most highly specialized. The greatest intelligence and skill are called into play to produce special tools, and to render their use highly efficient.

The armies and navies of the European nations and of Japan are trained, just as college athletes are trained for boat-racing, baseball, football, and competitive contests of the gymnasium. The personnel is kept in the pink of condition for prompt and decisive individual effort and also for supreme collective effort in team work.

A pugilist finds it necessary to train with the most complete thoroughness to get himself into prime condition for a fight, while his opponent is training in the same manner. When they meet, it is not the strength, skill, and endurance of the normal man that counts in the fight, but it is the supernormal manhood that has been added to the normal man. An ordinary untrained citizen, although he may possess undeveloped resources equal to those of the trained pugilist, would have no chance whatever in a fight with him.

Similarly, such an army and a navy as we should be able to improvise in time of war would have no more chance of success against an army and fleet of a European nation or of Japan than the average citizen would have with a skilled, toughened, and hardened pugilist.

There is one source of our naval weakness that of itself alone may bring disaster. It is incomprehensible that such a condition should be allowed to exist. When a fleet goes into distant waters, it should have a nearby base. We have neither the coaling stations nor the dry-docks and harbors of refuge that are absolutely indispensable to the fleet of a country with world pretensions.

It is absolutely vital that we should be able to defend the Panama Canal, but we have no dry-docks or efficient repair-shops there, and we have none within a thousand miles of there.

A couple of million dollars well spent to remedy this defect might, Admiral Knight declares, very conceivably double the efficiency of the fleet in a critical emergency by making it possible for every ship to go out in perfect condition.

We have capable naval bureaus of Ordnance, Construction, and Repair, and for the direction of personnel; but these bureaus are not responsible for the readiness of the fleet for war. Admiral Knight suggests a remedy. He says:

"This is the last and great defect in the efficiency of the Navy. How shall it be remedied? The answer is, I think, by the creation in the Navy Department of a 'Division of Strategy and Operations' preferably not co-equal with the present Bureaus but superior to them and standing be-

tween them and the Secretary. This arrangement would be a recognition of the fact that all the activities of the present Bureaus should lead up to the Secretary through a channel which coördinates them all and directs them toward war efficiency.

"The title proposed for the new office: DIVISION OF STRATEGY AND OPERATIONS, *covers very completely the ground that I have in mind. As standing for Strategy this Division would plan what to do; and as standing for Operations, it would direct the execution of its plans. It would correspond more or less closely with the General Staff of the Army and the First Sea Lord of the British Admiralty, whose duties are thus defined:*

"1. Preparation for war: All large questions of naval policy and maritime warfare—to advise. 2. Fighting and seagoing efficiency of the fleet, its organization and mobilization, including complements of ships as affecting total numbers, system of gunnery and torpedo exercises of the fleet, and tactical employment of air-craft, and all military questions connected with the foregoing; distribution and movements of all ships in commission and in reserve. 3. Superintendence of the War Staff and the Hydrographic Department."

THE NEEDS OF OUR NAVY

George von Lengerke Meyer, former Secretary of the Navy, has many times in recent years called attention to the fact that a large proportion of the money appropriated for the upbuilding and up-keep of our Navy has been misapplied to the building and up-keep of useless navy yards.

During the first fifteen years of the present century, we spent $1,656,000,000 on our Navy, while during the same period Germany spent $1,137,-000,000.

Notwithstanding the fact that during this period Germany spent 31 per cent. less money on her navy than we did on ours, she has a more powerful navy than we have. This difference represents a sum of more than half a billion of dollars. With that amount of money we could have built two super-dreadnoughts a year, for the past fifteen years, costing $15,000,000 each, with $60,000,000 to spare for battle-cruisers, destroyers, and submarines. In short, had we spent our naval appropriations as economically as have the Germans during the past fifteen years, we might have had thirty more battleships than we now have, all super-dreadnoughts of the *Queen Elizabeth* type, the latest and most powerful pattern. This number of up-to-date super-dreadnoughts would have far more than doubled the battle

[175]

strength of our Navy. We should have out-classed England in battleship strength.

The following facts are so pregnant and so important and so ably expressed that I can do no better than to give them in Mr. Meyer's own words:

"Until within a few years no naval appropriation could pass the Senate which did not meet the sanction of both a Northern and Southern Senator, each of whom was a member of the Committee on Naval Affairs. It is interesting, in consequence, to analyze some of the appropriations between 1895 and 1910.

"In 1899 a site was purchased in Frenchman's Bay, Maine, at a cost of $24,650—far above the assessed valuation—and later an additional amount of $600,000 was expended to obtain there an absolutely unnecessary coaling-station, which has since been dismantled, as it was practically unused.

"At the Portsmouth Navy Yard, so called, in Kittery, Maine, a dock was built at an expense of $1,122,800, and later it was found necessary to blast away rock in the channel in order to reach the dock, at an additional expense of $745,300.

"Between 1895 and 1910 improvements, machinery, repairs, and maintenance in the yard amounted to $10,857,693, although there was a large navy-yard within seventy miles.

"*On the other hand, at Port Royal, South Carolina, a dock was built at the insistence of the Southern Senator, at a cost of $450,000, which proved useless, and, although the original cost of the site was but $5,000, it was not abandoned as a naval base until $2,275,000 had been expended.*

"*Not the least daunted by this extravagant waste, the same Senator determined to have a share of the naval melon for his State, so, with the assistance of the Northern Senator, he obtained the establishment of another naval station at Charleston, South Carolina, in 1901. There was no strategic value thus accomplished, nor was it necessary, with the Norfolk Navy-Yard located at Hampton Roads. The $5,000,000 which has been squandered at Charleston includes a dry-dock built for battleships, costing $1,250,000, but which experience shows can only be used by torpedo-boat destroyers and gunboats. The $5,000,-000 could have been employed to great advantage at the Norfolk Navy-Yard, where the battleship fleet generally assembles. A portion even could have been used wisely at Key West, Florida, a supplementary base of real strategic value for torpedoes and submarines—a protection to the Gulf of Mexico and the mouth of the Mississippi River, and on account of its geographical situation, Key West would serve as a base of supplies to the fleet in the Caribbean Sea.*

"*The purpose of the navy-yards is to keep the*

*fleet in efficient condition. Their location should
be determined by strategic conditions, their number by the actual needs of the fleet. The maintenance of navy-yards which do not contribute to
battle efficiency is a great source of waste.*

*"The United States has over twice as many
first-class navy-yards as Great Britain, with a
navy more than double the size of ours, and more
than three times as many as Germany, whose navy
is larger than that of the United States.*

*"The total cost of navy-yards up to June 30th,
1910, with land, public works, improvements, machinery, and maintenance, including repairs,
amounts to $320,600,000.*

*"Overburdened with a superfluous number of
navy-yards distributed along the Atlantic coast
from Maine to Louisiana, in 1910 I recommended
that Congress give up and dispose of naval stations at New Orleans, Pensacola, San Juan, Port
Royal, New London, Sackett's Harbor (New
York), Culebra, and Cavité, none of which was a
first-class station. The average yearly cost of
maintaining these stations between 1905 and 1910
was $1,672,675, and very little useful work had
been performed at any of them. Later, I practically closed them, but could not abolish or dispose of them, no action having been taken by Congress. Pensacola and New Orleans have since
been reopened by my successor.*

THE NEEDS OF OUR NAVY

"The interests of the country and the interests of the Navy would be best served by one first-class naval base with sufficient anchorage for the entire fleet, north of the Delaware, equipped for docking, repairing, etc., and another station of equal capacity at Norfolk, in Chesapeake Bay, with Guantanamo, Cuba, to serve as the winter-station rendezvous.

"On the Pacific coast we are fortunate in having only two naval stations, one at Bremerton, on Puget Sound, established in 1891, with ample depth of water, costing to date about $9,000,000; and the other at Mare Island, established in 1850, some thirty miles from the harbor of San Francisco, with inadequate depth and width of water along its water-front. The total costs, with maintenance and repairs, have amounted to $35,000,- 000, and, on account of insufficient depth of water, none of the battleships built in the last eight years could have been berthed there. . . .

"Building battleships without an adequate force of men is equal to wasting money; only ten ships of the first line and eleven of the second, according to the Navy Department, can be placed in full commission for service, due to a shortage of men and officers.

"To provide a proper complement for all vessels of the Navy which could still be made useful would require an additional force of 18,556 men and 933 line officers, according to the testimony

of Admiral Badger before the Naval Committee, December 8, 1914.

"That we have not been getting proper return for money expended in the Navy is not known to the majority of our people, nor is it realized to what extent political influences have misdirected the appropriations during the past twenty-five years. The remedy will only come from absolute publicity.

"Let a special committee be appointed to investigate the conditions in the Navy.

"Let a special committee of military experts from the Army and Navy be appointed to recommend what naval stations shall be abolished and sold and if any shall be established to take their places.

"Let Congress inaugurate a national council of defense made up of members of the Cabinet, Senate, and House, with the chiefs of staff from the Army and Navy, that more efficient co-operation may be obtained between the executive and legislative branches of the Government in respect to military requirements.

"Let Congress establish a general staff in the Navy."

CHAPTER VII

LANGUAGE OF THE BIG GUNS

IN the present war, the big guns, both on land and sea, have told their own story, and they have commanded conviction of their usefulness in proportion to the loudness of their voice.

Following the introduction of armor-plate by Ericsson's *Monitor* and the *Merrimac,* armor-plate was answered by increasing the size of guns and projectiles. Brown prismatic powder was developed to slow the burning and lessen the initial pressure, thereby securing a better maintenance of pressure behind the projectile in its passage along the bore of the gun.

Guns weighing more than a hundred tons were built in England for the use of brown prismatic powder, but it was found that, after firing a few rounds, the guns drooped at the muzzle under the shock of discharge, and lost their accuracy.

The invention and development of smokeless gunpowder, mainly during the ten years between 1887 and 1897, resulted in radical improvements in guns of all calibers.

Only about 44 per cent. of the products of combustion of the old black powder and the brown prismatic powder were gaseous. The balance, about 56 per cent., were solid matter, and produced smoke. It will be seen, at a glance, that smokeless powder, whose products of combustion are entirely gaseous, possesses enormous ballistic advantages, quite independent of its smokelessness. Less than half the products of combustion of the old smoke-producing powders being gaseous, much energy was absorbed from the gases, to heat and vaporize the solid products constituting the smoke. Additional heat was consumed by the work of expelling the smoke from the gun.

The products of combustion of smokeless powder are not only practically all gaseous, but also they are much hotter than the products of combustion of the old, smoky, black powder. Owing to this fact, smokeless powder may be considered about four times as powerful as the old black powder.

When a projectile is thrown from a gun, although it is not heated appreciably, yet heat-energy represented by its velocity is absorbed from the expanding gases of the powder charge. When a 12-inch projectile weighing a thousand pounds is thrown from one of our long naval guns, it has a striking energy, fifty feet from the muzzle, of about 50,000 foot-tons—that is to say, it strikes with a force equal to that of 50,000 tons falling from a height of one foot, or one ton falling from a height of 50,000 feet. As the 12-inch naval gun weighs about 50 tons, the energy absorbed from the gases in the shape of velocity of the projectile is sufficient to lift a thousand 12-inch guns to a height of one foot.

As a projectile weighs half a ton, the force of the blow is about the same as though the projectile were to be dropped from a height of twenty miles, with no deduction for the resistance of the atmosphere.

When the projectile is stopped, a quantity of heat is re-developed exactly equal to that absorbed from the powder gases in giving the projectile its high velocity; and the quantity of heat absorbed from the powder gases in throwing a thousand-pound projectile from our big naval guns is sufficient to melt 750 pounds of cast iron, which is enough to heat the projectile white hot.

Obviously, when the projectile strikes armor-plate, either the plate or the projectile must yield, for the reason that the projectile brings to bear upon a 12-inch plate an energy sufficient to fuse a hole right through it, and this is substantially what it does. The hard and toughened steel of the plate is heated and softened by the force of impact, and, although the projectile may be cold after it has passed through, it actually does fuse a hole through the plate, the metal flowing like wax from its path.

The introduction of smokeless cannon-powder was followed by a recession from guns of great weight and caliber, to guns of smaller weight and smaller caliber, the aim being to make up for the greater smashing power of huge projectiles, thrown at a lower velocity, with projectiles of smaller size, thrown at much greater velocity and having a greater power of penetration of armor-plate, which was constantly being made thicker and tougher and harder in order to resist the impact of armor-piercing projectiles.

As armor-plate continued to increase in thickness and in powers of resistance, guns of bigger and bigger caliber had to be made, capable of withstanding the enormous pressure necessary to throw projectiles of sufficient size and at sufficiently high velocity to penetrate any armor-plate that could be opposed to them.

With every improvement in armor-plate, the gun and the projectile have been improved and enlarged, until now no armor-plate carried by any ship can withstand the naval guns of largest caliber. In its race with armor-plate, the gun has thus far been the winner.

The victory of the *Monitor* over the *Merrimac* at Hampton Roads, half a century ago, was far less decisive than was the victory of armor-plate over the gun of that time.

The whole world well remembers the story of how the *Monitor* arrived in the nick of time, and saved the Federal fleet from destruction. But the salvation of the Northern fleet was of little advantage, for the advent of the *Monitor* rendered obsolete and useless every warship of every fleet in the world.

Great Britain found herself without a navy. There was universal consternation. It was a world-wonder that no government had before resorted to so simple an expedient, and one whose utility was so very evident.

It must be remembered that the guns of that period were muzzle-loading smooth-bores, and that the round, solid projectiles thrown by them were intended merely to knock holes in the sides of wooden warships and to pound down the walls of brick or stone forts. Bombshells were then thin, hollow spheres of cast iron, charged with black gunpowder, and they were not intended for penetration, their destructiveness depending upon the fragments hurled by their explosion, or upon their ignition of inflammable material.

It is a curious phase of human progress that what is old and tried is venerated and conserved with solicitous regard out of all proportion to merit. Innovations must not only have evident merit, but their merit must also be so indubitably proven by application and use as to replace the old and revered, in spite of the opposition of over-zealous conservatism. The substitution of the sail for the galley-slave was a very slow process, until it received especial stimulus in the fierce forays of the marauding Northmen and the raids of the

Mediterranean corsairs. Similarly, did the sail slowly give way to steam.

A modern wooden steam-launch or a forty-foot motor-boat, with cedar sides, driven by gasolene-engines and armed with a single three-and-a-half-inch gun, would be able today to attack and destroy the famous *Monitor* of Ericsson, in spite of its armor-plate, for the reason that the launch or motor-boat would have vastly greater speed, and also for the reason that its gun would have vastly greater range, and would be able to penetrate the soft iron armor of the *Monitor* with projectiles charged with a high explosive to explode inside. The motor-boat, lying outside the range of the huge 11-inch guns of the *Monitor*, could hold a position of perfect safety during the conflict, and, by consequence, would need no armored protection.

Thus we see that the sufficiency of armor-plate must, other things being equal, inevitably depend upon insufficiency in range and penetrating power of the gun to which it is opposed. An unarmored vessel, with guns capable of penetrating the armor-plate of an opponent having shorter-range guns, needs only to have superior speed in order to choose a position out of range of the armor-clad's guns, and, atmospheric conditions being favorable, to destroy it without itself being exposed to any danger whatsoever.

But there are other conditions which prevent the

gun, however long its range and however great its power of penetration, from being a complete defense in the absence of armored protection. These conditions are—the limit of vision due to the rotundity of the earth, even in clear weather, the limitation of vision, at much nearer distances, in thick or hazy weather, and, of course, the greatly increased difficulty of hitting at extreme ranges. Also, it is necessary to be able to observe, from the fighting-tops, where trial shots strike, in order to get the correct range, and lay the guns exactly upon the target.

In the recent North Sea fight, firing began at more than 17,000 yards, or about ten miles; 12-inch and 13-inch shells from the British ships struck the *Bluecher* before more than the upper works of the *Bluecher* could be seen from the decks of the British ships. Only by the fire-control officers, a hundred feet above the decks, could her whole hull be seen. When the first huge shells came plunging down out of the sky upon the *Bluecher,* her gunners could not see the ships from which they came.

It is true that with much more powerful guns than those of her enemy, an unarmored vessel would be able to shoot right through any armored protection opposed to them. But there is the danger that an armored ship of an enemy may emerge from the fog or haze, or from out of the darkness at night, and then neither speed nor weight of gun-fire might save the unarmored ship.

The unarmored vessel would not be able with her small guns, if she carried them, materially to injure her armored enemy, whereas the enemy, with its secondary batteries, firing with enormous rapidity and faster than the speed of the heavier guns, would be able to riddle her in a few moments. Consequently, it is considered wise to employ sufficient armor to afford protection against the rapid-fire guns of smaller caliber. Such armor also at longer ranges affords considerable protection against the big guns, for it must be expected that not all projectiles will strike the plate at right angles. They strike at all angles, and sometimes at very sharp angles, and glance off, in which case armor of moderate thickness may save a ship by diverting the shots, while, if she were wholly unarmored, she might be destroyed.

We may then conclude that an ideal fighting ship would be one having very great speed, carrying very large and powerful guns, and protected by armor-plate of but moderate thickness. Actually, such a ship is the modern battle-cruiser. We have as yet not one of these ships in our Navy, while the Japanese have two of the most powerful in the world, and more building; England has eight, and more building; Germany has four, and more building.

The first improvements following the advent of armor-plate were made, as might be supposed, in

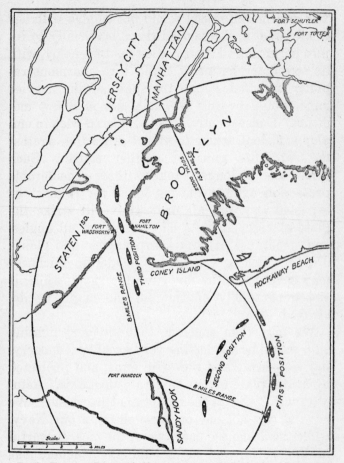

How the Fleet of an Enemy with fifteen-inch guns could Bombard and Destroy Forts
Hancock, Hamilton and Wadsworth, and also all of Brooklyn and part of Manhattan,
from a position beyond the range of the Guns of those Forts; also showing how, after Fort
Hancock is destroyed, the Fleet could move yet nearer for the Destruction of Forts Hamilton and Wadsworth, and still be out of range of those Forts, and finally, after their Destruction, how it could Bombard New York, Jersey City and Brooklyn at Short Range.

the gun and in the projectile. The old smooth-bore, with spherical projectile, was replaced by the breech-loading rifle and the conical projectile having a copper driving ring and gas-check, by which a projectile possessing enormously greater mass for its caliber could be hurled at much higher velocity and kept point on.

Extraordinary improvements have been continuously made in armor-plate, to harden and toughen it and to give it greater powers of resistance, while battleships have been made larger and larger to support heavier and heavier armor-plate. Nevertheless, the first improvement in guns and projectiles that followed the advent of the armor-clad, gave the gun the lead, and the gun has kept the lead ever since.

Today, the long-range, high-power naval gun, charged with smokeless powder, and throwing a projectile made of tempered steel inconceivably tough and hard, and charged with high explosive, is the most powerful dynamic instrument ever produced by man. A 12-inch naval gun throws a projectile weighing half a ton, at a velocity nearly three times the speed of sound. A charge of three hundred and seventy-five pounds of smokeless powder, strong as dynamite, is employed for the projectile's propulsion.

It may be safely assumed that at fighting ranges the residual velocity of a 12-inch, armor-piercing, half-ton projectile, thrown from one of the most powerful 12-inch naval guns, develops heat enough upon impact to fuse its way through 12-inch plate.

When a solid body comes into collision with another solid body, the energy of motion is instantly converted into heat, except such portion of it as may be consumed in fragmentation, and retained in the motion of the flying pieces. If two armor-plates, twelve inches in thickness, could be brought together face to face, each with a velocity equal to that of a modern 12-inch projectile, the energy of the impact would be sufficient to melt both plates.

New suns are created by the occasional collision of great celestial bodies in their flight through space. The heat generated by such collisions is, however, vastly greater than that developed by the collision of a projectile against armor-plate, for the reason that the velocity of celestial bodies is so much greater, being commonly from thirty-five to fifty miles per second, and sometimes as high as two hundred miles per second, instead of but three-quarters of a mile per second. The heat developed by the collision of worlds is sufficient not only to fuse them, but also to gasefy them, and reduce them to their ultimate elements. All the suns that emblazon the evening sky have been created in this manner, and the heat generated by their natal impact is sufficient to maintain their radiant energy for hundreds of millions of years. Planets are born, some of them to become inhabited worlds, finally to grow old and die, with the extinguishment of all life upon them, while their parent sun is still blazing hot.

The earth is being constantly bombarded with meteorites, usually of very small size. But the earth is armor-plated with its envelope of air. The impact of meteorites upon this envelope, at the enormous speed at which they are traveling through space, is fatal to them, and they are dashed to pieces and consumed upon it, as though it were a solid shield of hardest tempered steel. It is seldom, indeed, that a meteorite has sufficient size and mass to penetrate through the atmosphere to the earth's surface. Were it not for the protection offered by the earth's envelope of air, every living thing upon its surface would be very soon destroyed by the meteoric bombardment from the heavens. A minute particle of meteoric dust, traveling at celestial velocity, would be more deadly than a bullet from a shoulder-rifle.

When a projectile is fired from a gun, it encounters the same atmospheric resistance, in proportion to its velocity and mass, as is encountered by a meteorite, the resistance increasing in a ratio something like the square of the velocity. When a battleship fires a 12-inch shot at another war-vessel ten miles away, the velocity is greatly reduced during flight, for an enormous amount of energy is consumed in punching a 12-inch hole ten miles long through the atmosphere. Gravitation, also, is drawing the projectile toward the earth with a constant pull of half a ton, to counteract which the trajectory must be made an upward curve. This makes the path longer, and consumes additional energy in raising the projectile to the top of the trajectory.

If a projectile could be thrown from a gun at a velocity equal to that of a meteor, it would blaze like the sun during flight, for the metal upon its surface would be fused and gasefied by the resistance and friction of the air. It would not make any difference whether it were made of the toughest, hardest tempered steel, or whether it were made of soft iron. The velocity would be so great that it would pass through the heaviest armorplate without appreciable reduction of speed. If the projectile were of lead, it would require armorplate of a greater thickness to stop it than if it were of steel, for the reason that its mass or weight for its bulk would be greater.

Distance and the intervening air are our most efficient protection. No armored defense now employed is wholly effectual, except the range be long. By consequence, then, future naval battles will be decided more and more by speed and size of guns, rather than by armored protection.

Were two modern dreadnoughts to battle at as close range as did the *Monitor* and the *Merrimac*, immediate destruction would be mutual. They would cripple each other more in four minutes than did the *Monitor* and the *Merrimac* in the four long hours during which they pounded each other.

The *Alabama* and *Kearsarge* fought for more than an hour, within bowshot of each other, before the *Alabama* was destroyed. Were two of the biggest and most heavily armored battleships in the world to fight today at as close range, one or the other of them would be destroyed in a very few minutes.

The projectiles fired from the monster naval guns now weigh many times as much as those thrown from the guns of either the *Monitor* or the *Merrimac,* and these huge projectiles have also a multiplied velocity. The total thickness of the armor of the *Monitor's* turret was ten inches. An iron wall of the character used in Ericsson's turret, five feet in thickness, would not afford adequate protection against our modern, monster guns.

Of course, the character of armor-plate has been vastly improved since that time. Instead of being merely soft iron, as was that of the *Monitor,* armor-plate is now made of the hardest and toughest tempered steel that science can produce. So, also, is the projectile. The projectile has far more than held its own. It is necessary, therefore, that the most heavily armored ships, as well as those unarmored, must fight today at long range, depending mainly upon skilled marksmanship and power and range of guns, rather than upon armored protection. A battle at close range between two huge modern dreadnoughts would be as deadly to both combatants as a duel between two men standing close together, face to face, holding pistols at each other's breast.

When a chemical engineer makes an invention, and needs money for its exploitation, he first interests capitalists by letting them see the invention practised on a laboratory scale, embodying essentially the same conditions as would be involved in the larger commercial application. Similarly, we may get a very just and dependable idea of the relative efficiency of guns and armor-plate on a naval-battle scale, by taking into consideration what would be the result of a lesser conflict, embodying essentially the same conditions.

Suppose two men were to fight a duel, one wearing armor capable of protecting him as efficiently against rifle balls as the heaviest armor carried by any warship today is capable of protecting it against modern cannon-fire; the other wearing no armor, and being thereby enabled to run much faster than his armor-clad opponent. Obviously, if the unarmored man had a gun of longer range than that carried by the protected man, he would be able to keep out of range of his enemy's gun, while still keeping him well within range. Thus he would be able to continue firing at him until he killed him, without in return being hit at all.

At the battle of Santiago, the American fleet made only about two per cent. of hits with its 12-inch guns. Since that time very great improvements have been made in fire-control, and the accuracy of gun-fire. Today, a battle-cruiser, going at the rate of thirty knots, will hit an object on the sky-line a tenth the size of a battleship with the accuracy that Buffalo Bill from horseback would hit a man's hat at a distance of twenty paces.

In the naval battle between von Spee and Cradock, off the coast of Chili, they opened fire on each other with deadly effect at 12,000 yards. In the running fight off the Falkland Islands, most of the execution was done at a range of 15,000 yards.

In the North Sea fight, according to the report of Admiral Beatty, the British shots began to take effect on the enemy at ten miles, and the whole battle was fought at a range of over seven miles. The German guns, being mounted so that they could be elevated much more than the British, were able to shoot not only as far, but even farther. The British guns, however, were much more effective, because of the greater weight of metal thrown.

When projectiles are increased in size the atmospheric resistance at equal velocity increases as the square of the diameter, while the mass increases as the cube of the diameter. Consequently, large projectiles lose less velocity during flight, in proportion to their weight, due to the resistance of the air, than do smaller projectiles.

Only within the last few years has rapid-fire with very large guns become possible. Now, however, loading machinery has been so perfected that the limit is no longer that of hand-power. Wherever in nature forces are opposed, there is a tendency toward an equilibrium. There is now a tendency toward the establishment of an equilibrium between the power of offense and the power of defense—between gun-fire and armor-plate.

Nevertheless, the mean force of gun-fire remains still far superior to that of armored resistance. The mean armored resistance is now about on a par with that of the moderate caliber guns, as, for example, 6- and 8-inch guns. If there were no larger guns than those of 6- and 8-inch caliber, guns and armor-plate would be about neck and neck in the race. Consequently, we must look to the winning of naval victories by the employment of guns of more than 8-inch caliber.

Speed is of such supreme importance in naval engagements that its value should be especially emphasized. Superior speed enables the fleet possessing it to choose its own position, thus determining the range and the direction from which the attack shall be made. If the fleet happens to have guns of larger caliber and longer range than the enemy, it may be important, also, to choose its weather by keeping out of action until it can

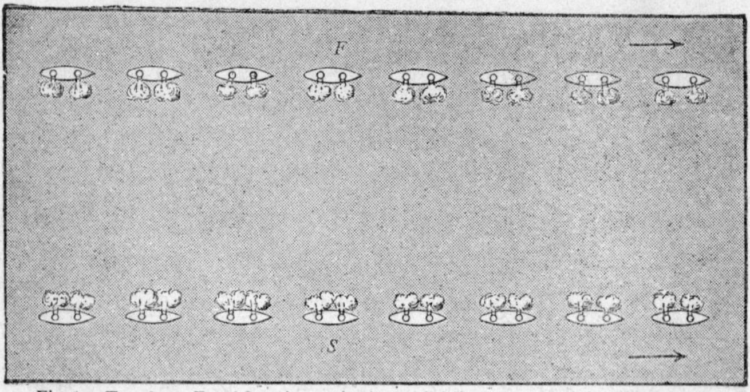

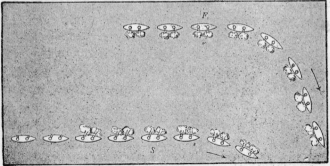

Fig. 1.—Two fleets, F and S, go into action in parallel lines, the range being chosen by the fleet, F, having ships of greatest speed and guns of longest range.

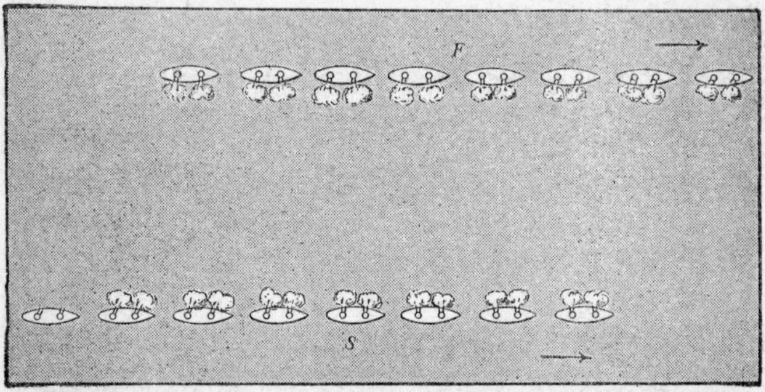

Fig. 2.—The faster fleet, F, forges ahead, concentrating the fire of both its front ships on the van ship of the slow fleet, while the rear ship of fleet S is thrown out of range and out of action.

Fig. 3.—The faster fleet, F, bends its course in front of the slower fleet, S, with increased concentration of fire on the leading ships of the latter, throwing its two rear ships out of action.

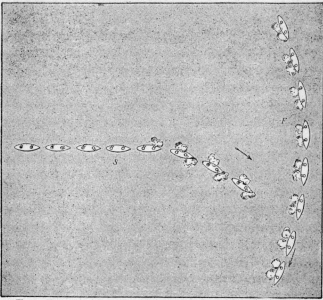

Fig. 4.—*The faster fleet, F, doubles around and crumples the slower fleet, S, and pours into its foremost ships an overwhelming enfilading fire, while its four rear ships are thrown out of action.*

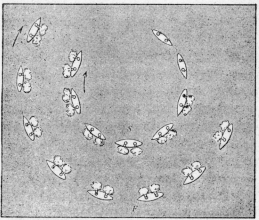

Fig. 5.—*The slower fleet, S, is forced into a circular position and destroyed, while its rear ships are constantly kept out of action.*

fight at the maximum range of its own guns. The slow fleet must always fight at a disadvantage.

Let us picture two opposing fleets drawn up for battle. The fleet with fastest ships and guns of longest range, lining up at the maximum effective distance for its fire, steams at first in a line parallel with the enemy and in the same direction that the enemy is steaming. The faster fleet is soon able to run its van ships forward of the van ships of the enemy, turning in front of them, thereby bringing the front ship of the enemy's line under the combined fire of its own two foremost ships, while the rearmost ship in its line of battle gets out of range of the rearmost ship of the enemy, placing the latter entirely out of action. This movement is continued until the enemy's line is encircled, crumpled up, and destroyed. Therefore, we see that superior speed enables the fleet possessing it to put a portion of an enemy's fleet entirely out of action, while at the same time placing the remainder of the enemy's ships under the combined fire of a superior number.

In June, 1897, I delivered a lecture before the Royal United Service Institution of Great Britain, in which I illustrated and recommended the employment of a gun of very large caliber for use on fighting ships and in coast fortifications.

The United States government had, several years previously, adopted the multi-perforated smokeless cannon-powder invented by me. This form of grain rendered it possible to use a pure nitro-cellulose smokeless powder in large guns, because it greatly reduced the initial area of combustion in proportion to the mass, while as the combustion progressed this condition was reversed and a very large area was presented to the flame of combustion in proportion to the mass. Consequently, the initial pressure in the gun was much reduced, while greater pressure was maintained behind the projectile in its flight through the gun than could be obtained by any other form of grain. This made possible the attainment of a very high velocity, with a comparatively low initial pressure and, consequently, with comparatively small strain upon the gun. For this reason, and because of the low heat in the combustion of pure nitro-cellulose powder, the erosive action upon the gun was reduced to a minimum.

I invented another and a special form of multi-perforated grain by means of which a yet lower initial pressure for a given density of loading was secured, the rate of combustion being still more highly accelerated.

Believing that the advantages of projectiles of great size, carrying a very large bursting charge, could be better illustrated by a gun of extraordinary caliber, I designed a cannon having a caliber of twenty-four inches, but having a weight of only 43 tons, the weight and length of the gun being the same as the British 12-inch 43-ton gun. This gun was designed to throw a semi-armor-piercing projectile weighing 1,700 pounds, and carrying an explosive charge of 1,000 pounds, the total weight of the projectile being 2,700 pounds. While the projectile was not designed to pierce heavy armor, it was capable of penetrating the decks and sides of light-armored cruisers and deep into earth or concrete for the destruction of forts. It was a veritable aërial torpedo. By means of the special form of multi-perforated smokeless powder designed for this gun, the huge projectile could be thrown to a distance of nine miles with the gun at maximum elevation, and still with a comparatively low chamber pressure.

The projectile was provided with a safety delay-action detonating fuse, designed to explode it after having penetrated the object struck, thereby securing the maximum destructive effects.

It is reported that the Germans have made a huge howitzer weighing 45 tons, having a caliber of $23\frac{1}{2}$ inches, which also is capable of throwing a projectile weighing more than a ton to a distance of nine miles.

The drawings used in my lecture were published in the *Journal of the Royal United Service Institution,* April, 1898, and re-published in many scientific and engineering magazines, and in newspapers both here and abroad. The descriptions of this gun and projectile were illustrated, as was the manner of its employment for the destruction of the kinds of forts destroyed by the Germans at Liège and Namur.

The use of high explosives in big armor-piercing projectiles is now universal, but on the publication of my lecture in 1897 I was subjected to much criticism, especially in some of the London newspapers, whose editors took issue with me as to the practicability of throwing large bursting charges of high explosives from high-power guns. Prior to that time the only success achieved in throwing large charges of high explosives was by use of the Zalinski pneumatic dynamite gun, a battery of which had been made and mounted at great expense at Sandy Hook. These air-guns imparted a maximum velocity of only about 600 feet per second to the projectile. The maximum charge was 600 pounds of nitro-gelatin. The projectile had no penetrating power whatsoever, and was designed to go off on impact.

My proposition to throw large charges of a high explosive from a big gun, at high velocity, using a propelling charge of gunpowder, appeared to many to be a very hare-brained intention indeed, to say nothing of shooting it through armor and exploding it behind the plate.

On my return to America in 1898, I laid the matter before General A. R. Buffington, Chief of the Bureau of Ordnance, United States Army, and Admiral Charles O'Neil, Chief of the Bureau of

Ordnance, United States Navy. General Buffington sent me to Sandy Hook, where my new explosive, Maximite, was subjected to a very thorough trial. The first 12-inch projectile charged with it was buried in sand in an armor-cased cellar, and exploded. More than seven thousand fragments of the projectile were recovered, being sifted out of the sand. Twelve-inch projectiles charged with Maximite were repeatedly fired through 12-inch armor-plate without exploding. Later, similar projectiles, armed with a fuse, were fired through the same plate and were exploded behind the plate. Although Maximite was fifty per cent. stronger than ordinary dynamite, yet it was so insensitive to shock as to be incapable of being exploded without the use of a very strong detonator. Maximite was the first high explosive successfully to be fired through heavy armor-plate, and exploded behind the plate, with a delay-action fuse. The fuse employed at that time was the invention of an army officer. Later, my fuse was subjected to a very long series of tests, and it was finally adopted in 1907 as the service detonating fuse by the United States Navy.

If Uncle Sam would listen with an understanding mind to the language of the big guns now speaking on land and sea, he would immediately build a large number of huge howitzers. He would build a large number of good roads, capable of standing the tread of these howitzers. He would build as well a goodly number of battle-cruisers, as big and as fast as any afloat in foreign seas, and armed with guns ranging as far as the guns of any foreign power.

CHAPTER VIII

AËRIAL WARFARE

IN the present European War is being tested
the enginery of destruction and slaughter
that has been building and accumulating for
half a century. It is the most stupendous experiment that the human race has ever tried. The
magnitude of it confounds the senses; the horror
obsesses the mind and stumps realization.

The influence of improvements in all kinds of
weapons and machinery of war is further and
further to complicate strategics. The more that
invention, science, and discovery are employed
in the development and perfection of implements
of war, the more the use of those implements
requires high inventive genius and high scientific
skill.

Before the outbreak of the war there were
many military engines awaiting a practical trial
in actual service, among them the dirigible balloon. During a period of forty years the nations
of the world have been obliged to do a good deal
of guessing, in spite of calculations based on
previous experience in wars whose mechanism
was very simple and crude as compared with the

[203]

present engines of war. But the improvements in weapons employed on terra firma did not constitute so far a step away from experience as engines of aërial warfare. Those engines of war which have been mainly the subjects of guesswork are the aëroplane and that dreadnought of the air, the Zeppelin, especially the latter. The advent of the aëroplane introduced an entirely new set of problems.

Before the advent of the aëroplane, the navigation of the air was confined to the balloon. Contrary to expectation, the aëroplane, instead of putting the balloon out of the race, served only to stimulate higher development of the balloon, with the result that the dirigible balloon and the aëroplane have been developed side by side.

From the outset, it was recognized that the chief desideratum in the development of the aëroplane consisted in greater stability, and especially in automatic equilibration.

The first aëroplanes were very imperfect. At the time of the early exhibitions which I witnessed, it was necessary to plan them to take place in the calm of the evening, just before sundown. The aëroplane could not go up in a wind. No aëronaut would have undertaken to go up except when there was no wind. Even a moderate breeze made them quite unmanageable. Now, however, the aëroplane can rise in a gale

of wind, and fly right into the teeth of a hurricane.

The old-style balloon could only go with the
wind. It could make no headway against it, but
had to float like a feather on the lightest breeze.
The modern dirigible, however, which has reached
its highest degree of perfection in the Zeppelin,
can travel through still air at a speed of sixty
miles an hour, the speed of a gale of wind, and
can brave a fifty-mile gale at a speed of ten miles
an hour. This is altogether remarkable when we
take into account the fact that the Zeppelin, with
all its load, must be lighter than air, and therefore, for its size, lighter than the fluffiest eider-
down.

LIMITATIONS OF THE AËRIAL BOMB

Aviation makes a strong appeal to the imagination, and this fact, together with errors and
misconceptions in the popular mind concerning
the use and power of high explosives, has led to
many strange predictions and weird conclusions
about the destruction which dirigibles and aëroplanes would be capable of doing by dropping
bombs from the sky.

Since the advent of aviation, many inventors
have directed their energies to aërial bombs and
bomb-dropping appliances. There have been,
from time to time, fearful forecasts of the de-

struction of warships, coast fortifications, and large cities; for it was claimed that air-craft would be able to drop explosive bombs capable of wrecking the heaviest battleship and of blowing up coast fortifications and utterly laying waste cities and towns. It was predicted that the aëroplane would be able, with its bombs, to scatter armies like chaff before the whirlwind.

The hopes of those who have believed in such dire destructiveness of bomb-dropping from aircraft have been dashed to the ground, with the bombs they have dropped. Of course, aviators may drop any form of infernal machine which, on exploding, will mangle by-standers with fragments of scrap iron, but the effect must necessarily be very local.

The most effective use aviators can make of bombs and infernal machines is to destroy one another in the sky and to attack magazines and storehouses, wireless stations, hangars, and balloon-sheds within the enemy's lines, and beyond the reach of other means of attack. Also, in connection with the attack of advancing troops, aërial bombs dropped from aëroplanes may be used with effect, especially in disentrenching an enemy. At sea, too, with the latest types of aëroplane, bombs of sufficient size and weight and power of penetration may be used destructively against unarmored or light-armored war-vessels. A more efficient means, however, than has yet been adopted is needed to secure the required accuracy. Naturally, such bombs are admirably adapted to the destruction of dirigible balloons. The swift-winged aviator is able to manœuvre at will around and above a huge dirigible and to attack it from any quarter.

There is probably no one subject about which there is more popular error than concerning the use and destructive effects of high explosives.

An anarchist once attempted to blow up London Bridge with two small sticks of dynamite, and succeeded merely in getting himself into trouble. At another time, a dynamiter entered the Houses of Parliament and exploded ten pounds of dynamite in one of the large corridors, with the result that it only made a hole in the floor and smashed a few windows.

As a matter of fact, airships are capable of working comparatively small damage by dropping bombs, unless the bombs can be made to hit and penetrate the object struck before exploding, for the reason that, unless confined, explosives have but little effect.

When a mass of high explosive is detonated upon a firm, resisting body, like the earth, or the deck of a battleship, or armor-plate, the effect is to rebound from the resisting body with small result. For example, when a mass of high explosive is set off on the earth's surface, the ball of incandescent gases bounds upward, spreading out in the form of an inverted cone. While it will blow a hole of considerable size into the ground, still the effect in a horizontal plane is practically nil. The windows of buildings standing in the vicinity of an explosion of this character are not blown inward, but are blown outward in the direction of the explosion by atmospheric reaction.

At Sandy Hook, several years ago, an experiment was tried with two hundred pounds of guncotton exploded against a twelve-inch plate, immediately back of which were placed a cage containing a rooster and a hen, and another cage containing a dog. The guncotton was hung against the plate and detonated. The effect upon the plate was nil. On examination, it was found that the dog and the two fowl had been made rather hard of hearing. That was the only noticeable effect upon the animals.

We all remember the test of the big, eighteen-inch Gathmann gun at Sandy Hook about twelve years ago, which threw a bomb containing six hundred pounds of compressed guncotton that was exploded against the face of a twelve-inch Kruppized plate. The first shot produced no visible effect except a yellow smudge on the face of the plate. It took three shots even to crack the plate and to shift it in its setting.

In competition with the Gathmann gun, a twelve-inch army rifle was fired against another plate of the same size and thickness and mounted in the same manner. The projectile contained only twenty-three pounds of Maximite. Yet, as the projectile penetrated the plate before the Maximite was exploded, a hole was blown through it a yard wide, and it was broken into several pieces.

These tests proved the effectiveness of even a small quantity of high explosive when properly confined, as by explosion after penetration, and the utter ineffectiveness of a large mass of high explosive when not confined or when exploded on the outside of a body.

Bombs carried by an airship and dropped upon the deck of a battleship may damage the superstructure a little, but they can have no material effect upon the ship itself, unless they are made heavy enough and strong enough, with the proper armor-piercing shape, and are dropped from a sufficient height to pierce the deck. Not unless the bomb can be made to penetrate an object before exploding can it effect much destruction.

At Santiago, the *Vesuvius,* with its pneumatic guns, threw several six-hundred-pound bombs, and exploded them on the Spanish fortifications, but the effect was wholly insignificant.

Several years ago, when the subway was being built, a dynamite magazine accidentally exploded in front of the Murray Hill Hotel. The magazine probably contained at least a ton of dynamite. A lot of windows were broken in the vicinity, some persons were injured, and a multitude badly scared, but the damage done even to the Murray Hill Hotel was comparatively small.

It has been predicted that Germany would send across the Channel a large fleet of airships and blow up British towns with the bombs that her great gas-bags might drop out of the heavens.

Now, at last, the much-vaunted and long-antici-pated Zeppelin invasion has come, and what is the result? Four peaceful citizens killed, and about ten thousand dollars' worth of property damage.

Let us suppose that the Germans should send a fleet of a hundred airships to drop bombs upon the city of London, returning to Germany each day for a new supply; and let us suppose that each airship should carry explosives enough to destroy two houses every day, which would be far more than they could actually average. Yet, if this aërial fleet should be able to destroy two hundred houses a day, or say, roughly, sixty thousand houses a year, it would succeed in destroying just about the annual growth of London, for that city has, during the past ten years, built sixty thousand new houses every year.

The dirigible balloon has one signal advantage over the aëroplane in the matter of bomb-dropping. It can both carry bigger bombs and remain stationary and hover while it drops them. With the aëroplane, however, there is necessarily great difficulty in hitting underlying objects, on account of the high speed at which it must travel to sustain flight. In order to float, an aëroplane must travel about thirty miles an hour. Even at this speed, it is moving forward at the rate of forty-four feet a second, and as a bomb travels at the same speed as the aëroplane, except for the retardation of the air, it moves forward forty-four feet the first second, while dropping sixteen feet. The next second the bomb falls sixty-four feet and moves forward forty-four feet, and so on.

Sixty miles an hour is a moderate speed for an aëroplane, however, and at that speed the bomb travels forward eighty-eight feet per second when it is dropped, so that, during the first second, while it descends but sixteen feet, it moves forward eighty-eight feet. It falls sixty-four feet the next second, and moves forward eighty-eight feet, and so on, descending in a parabolic curve, so that, by the time it strikes the earth, it may be several hundred feet from the place at which it is aimed.

Although the dirigible balloon, a Zeppelin, for example, may hover in a stationary position at will when dropping bombs, still it constitutes such an enormous target that it must fly very high in order to keep out of range of gun-fire. Guns are now made which can reach air-craft at the height of two miles. At that height, or at half that height, there can be but little accuracy in bomb-dropping, even from the stationary Zeppelin.

The efficiency of a fighting machine is exactly proportionate to the amount of life and property that it can destroy in a given time with the minimum exposure of property and life in order to do the work. If a fleet of a dozen Zeppelins should be able to attack and destroy an entire British fortified town like Dover, it would be a good investment. If, however, the loss that it would be able to inflict upon the enemy were only equal to the loss that the British would inflict upon it, then it would be a bad investment, or at least, an investment without profit, for the reason that, in war, it is poor policy to risk the destruction of a valuable war-engine merely for the destruction of what may be termed non-belligerent property of an enemy, such as the dwellings of the inhabitants of a city.

Suppose, for example, that a couple of Zeppelins should be able to destroy houses in a British town having a value ten times as great as the value of one of the Zeppelins, and, in the attack, should lose one of the Zeppelins, it would not be a profitable raid, for a Zeppelin, being useful for scouting purposes, is a potential factor in deciding the issue of the war, whereas the houses have practically no bearing on the issue of the war.

It is good policy to use both men and machinery of war only for the destruction of men and machinery of an enemy, and not for the destruction of non-combatant inhabitants and property.

Much has been said about gun-fire from aircraft upon underlying troops. A man standing on the earth, being seen endwise, presents a much smaller target to the vertical fire of the air-man than he presents when fired at horizontally from the earth, because in the one case he is seen end-to, and in the other case side-to. Besides, several other men may be exposed to the horizontal fire. The air-man, however, is a conspicuous target, and if his machine is hit and crippled the result is fatal to him.

Aëroplane and Dirigible Compared

As I have for many years predicted, the chief use of air-craft, whether aëroplane or dirigible balloon, is for purposes of reconnaissance.

This war has amply demonstrated the fact that air-craft are of enormous value. They have rendered surprises in force practically impossible. Each side has been able to keep itself fully aware of the numbers and disposition of opposing troops.

The aëroplane costs but a fraction of what the Zeppelin costs, while the Zeppelin presents a target enormously larger. It constitutes a target so big as to make the broad side of a barn blush with envy.

As one effective hit will bring down either aëroplane or Zeppelin alike, obviously, the aëroplane has the advantage over the Zeppelin, as a target, equal to the difference in size multiplied by the difference in cost. Furthermore, the aëroplane is far more mobile and more rapid in flight than the Zeppelin.

In judging of the value of the Zeppelin for purposes of reconnaissance on land, as compared with the aëroplane, we must take into account the fact that a large number of aëroplanes can be built for the cost of a single Zeppelin, and manned with the crew of a single Zeppelin, and that these many aëroplanes, operating in concert, will be able to do much more effective work than one Zeppelin.

If the Allies would be good enough not to shoot at them, Zeppelins might be very efficient indeed, hovering along the battle-front. These dirigibles have been very conspicuous for their absence from the battle-front in the war.

The use of the Zeppelin as a troop-ship has yet to be proven, and its value for the purpose will depend upon how it compares with the aëroplane for the same purpose. Aëroplanes capable of carrying at least a dozen soldiers each, with the arms and equipment of a raider's outfit, can now be built. Obviously, as a large number of such aëroplanes can be built at the cost of a single Zeppelin, and as the aëroplane can travel even faster than the Zeppelin, the Zeppelin cannot for one moment compare with the aëroplane, even for the purpose of carrying troops.

There is one purpose, however, for which the Zeppelin is admirably adapted, where it is much superior to the aëroplane, and it is for reconnaissance over sea. The Zeppelin can hang on the sky and scan the sea as a hawk scans a field for its prey; and as it can carry a wireless apparatus capable of transmitting messages to a distance of two hundred miles or more, it can keep the German fleet constantly informed of the positions of the British fleet in the near seas. It is thus able to direct a sortie of ships when the numbers and disposition of the enemy's ships are such as to insure success.

The Zeppelin has also a very important use in the detection of submarines, for the reason that from a vertical position submarines, under favorable conditions, can easily be seen at considerable depths below the surface, and the Zeppelin, with its long-range wireless, is able promptly to report such valuable information.

I am of the opinion that the Germans have planned and built their Zeppelins mainly for oversea fighting against England, and for a prospective invasion of England. I think they must have been disappointed in the lack of destructiveness that their bombs have had when dropped from Zeppelins, while the moral effect on England must also have been disappointing.

From the point of German advantage, it would be a good plan to frighten the British if it would take the fight out of them, but it is a very bad plan to frighten the British if it puts more fight into them. The Zeppelin raids have certainly had the effect of stimulating the British fighting spirit.

It is especially regrettable that the United States Government did not heartily co-operate with the Wright Brothers to lead the world in the development of the aëroplane; but nothing of the sort was done. "We have," as Congressman Gardner says, "been experimenting and expecting and reporting and contracting and considering—in fact, we have been doing everything except building aëroplanes."

The Wright Brothers, however, were received with glad foreign embrace. They were generously encouraged abroad, both by co-operative and competitive experiments and by liberal purchases. The result was that, on the breaking out of the European War, France, for example, had 1,400 aëroplanes, while the United States had but twenty-three, mostly obsolete. The United States Government has followed its time-honored custom of allowing its naval and military inventions to be developed and perfected abroad before adoption here.

Prior to the outbreak of the European War, this government ordered from abroad an up-to-date French aëroplane with two Salmson motors, and one of the latest German aëroplanes with two Mercedes motors, with the intention of building a few of these machines. Then came the European War. The American purchases were commandeered, and we were thereby prevented from acquiring the much-desired air-craft.

The de Bange obturator, an indispensable part of the breech mechanism of all large guns, was originally an American invention, but this Government allowed it to be developed and perfected abroad and given a foreign name.

Ericsson's *Monitor* was taken up by Europeans, right where its private builders left it, and it has been developed, mainly in England, into the modern super-dreadnought.

The interchangeable system of manufacture of small arms was developed and perfected in America, but received no encouragement from the government. This system is now universally employed in the manufacture of small arms, and also in the manufacture of all kinds of machinery. It is for this reason that we are able to get a spare part for an automobile that will fit in place perfectly without having it specially made. Before the advent of the interchangeable system of manufacture of firearms, a sportsman in England went to his gunsmith to be measured for a shotgun just as he went to his tailor to be measured for a suit of clothes. At that time, no two guns were made exactly alike, and no piece of one gun would fit any other gun, while now all the parts of one gun will fit in the places of corresponding parts in every other gun of the same pattern.

The year the United States Government adopted multi-perforated smokeless powder, Congress appropriated only $30,000 for smokeless powder, the orders to be divided among the different manufacturers. This meant that inventors, like myself, who had started in a small way, were driven out of business. I went to England with my multi-perforated smokeless-powder grain, which had been adopted by the United States Government, but found it hard to get foreign manufacturers to recognize either the superiority of the multi-perforated grain or of the pure nitrocellulose powder. The excessive erosion, however, of guns used in the present war, due to the use of powders containing a high percentage of nitroglycerin, is already making those countries using nitroglycerin powders look longingly to the superior smokeless powder used in the United States.

The United States Government has as yet taken no steps worth considering toward the obtainment of Zeppelins, or any other practical dirigible balloon. At the present time, there is not one in the American service.

At the outbreak of hostilities abroad, France had 22 dirigibles and 1,400 aëroplanes; Russia, 18 dirigibles and 800 aëroplanes; Great Britain,

9 dirigibles and 400 aëroplanes; Belgium, 2 dirigibles and 100 aëroplanes; Germany, 40 dirigibles and 1,000 aëroplanes; Austria, 8 dirigibles and 400 aëroplanes; while the United States had, as I have mentioned, only 23 aëroplanes, mostly obsolete.

Last year, the Secretary of the Navy appointed a Board to investigate the subject of aviation for the Navy, and to make recommendations. The Board recommended the appropriation of $1,300,-000 for that year, but Congress cut off the first left-hand numeral and appropriated the sum of $350,000 for the purpose.

The present war has demonstrated that aircraft are the eyes of both armies and navies. If the Wright Brothers could have come to the country's aid in the Spanish War, the American fleet would not have remained in doubt outside Santiago Harbor. Before the advent of aviation, one of the chief desiderata to a commanding officer was to find out what the enemy was doing behind the hill. Without the aëroplane, it is impossible to prevent surprises in force, and to avoid the deadly ambuscade. The aëroplane is absolutely indispensable for the location of masked batteries. It is impossible, without aëroplanes, even to approximate the number and disposition of troops to which an army may be opposed. It is necessary to have not only a sufficient number of aëroplanes, especially designed and equipped for this purpose, but also other aëroplanes, armed and equipped, to co-operate with them, and defend them against attack from the aëroplanes of the enemy. Just as dreadnoughts require battle-cruisers, and both require torpedo-boat destroyers, and all require other scout-ships and submarines, for co-operation against a fleet of an enemy, so do dirigibles and the different types of aëroplanes, according to their purpose, require one another for concert of action.

What we have already seen of battles fought in the sky leads us to surmise that aërial battles of the future will be fought on a much larger scale. It will be found that the commander who expects to conquer the ground held by an enemy must first conquer the sky. Aviation carries war into the third dimension.

Not only must the advance or retirement of troops be supported by artillery thundering from hill to hill, but also the troops must be supported and guided by pilots in the sky.

The last Congress appropriated $1,000,000 for the aviation purposes of the Navy. It is the same million dollars that was cut from last year's appropriation, which ought to have been expended for the purpose during that period.

It is a strange paradox that America, which has led the world in discovery and invention as applied to the industrial arts and sciences, should follow the rest of the world in their adoption by the Army and Navy. The trouble is not with the bureaus and boards of the Army and Navy, which have merely the power to recommend such things, but it is the fault of Congressional false economy. As long as we allow other nations to lead us, both in the character and quantity of naval and military equipment, we are destined always to be weaker than other nations in that equipment; consequently, when war comes, we spend money with the extravagance of frenzy to remedy the defect. We economized before the War of 1812, and during that war we wasted ten times as much as we had saved by our economy. We had disqualified ourselves by our economies to such an extent before the outbreak of the great Civil War that this conflict became one of the most deadly and most expensive in the history of the world. What we saved by our economies, compared to what we lost by them on that occasion, is like a drop of water to a river of water. But we failed to profit by the experience, and, when the Spanish War broke out, we spent money with all the lavishness of prodigal inefficiency.

If we could only be as wise as we have been lessoned by our sad experience, we would immediately take adequate measures to forefend ourselves against a repetition of such experiences; and one of those measures would be the building of an aërial fleet commensurate with our large needs.

CHAPTER IX

OUR ARMAMENTS NOT A BURDEN

LIFE being a reaction between the individual and environing stimuli, it naturally follows that those stimuli not destructive are necessarily formative.

The health and development of nations are governed by the same law that governs the health and development of individuals. When an individual is subjected to a burden that does not break him, or to a trial that he is able to master, he is strengthened, not weakened, by the burden or the trial. Every individual is constantly being attacked by microbes of disease. So long as he possesses sufficient powers of resistance to repel invasion of disease, his ability to resist disease is strengthened, and his immunity to further attacks is increased. It is only when disease gets inside a man that it becomes a destroyer.

It is not a bad thing for a hen, but, on the contrary, it is a very good thing for a hen to lay eggs and sit on them and hunger for three weeks in order to hatch the chicks, and then to scratch for them and hunt for them until they are able to take care of themselves. She is stronger, healthier, more intelligent, more competent, and altogether a better hen because of her exertion and her sacrifice. The rearing of her chicks imposes no burden on the farmer, because she gets the wealth for their growth out of the ground.

The human mother who bears and rears sons and daughters is supremely rewarded for all the pain and the burden. The husband and wife who toil for each other and their children are able to arrive thereby, and only thereby, at most complete living and the goal of supreme happiness. Happiness is our sense of the normal exercise of faculty; consequently happiness is the feel of normal life; unhappiness the feel of abnormal life.

Just as we are strengthened by bearing all burdens that are not so heavy as to crush us beneath their weight, so the nation is enriched by the burdens it bears and the expenditures it makes for the general welfare of its people. We may help our understanding of this matter by recognizing the truth that everything primarily comes out of the ground, and that whatever comes out of the ground, whether from agriculture or mining, is newly-created wealth. Whatever stimulates a more active development of our natural resources produces accordingly a proportionate amount of new wealth.

The people have been taught, until the belief is now well-nigh universal, that the cost of establishing, equipping, maintaining, and supporting a standing army, the cost of building, manning, and supporting a large navy, and the expense of manufacturing and storing large supplies of ammunition and other war-materials, represent just so much dead loss to the taxpayers of the country.

It is necessary to correct this error, and to disseminate the truth that the building of battleships, the manufacture of arms and ammunition, the manufacture of supplies of food and clothing, require large numbers of laborers and skilled artisans, who become a great market for food and supplies of every description for their convenience and comfort, thereby giving employment to myriads of others, back to the farmer; while the money paid for wages and produce is kept constantly in circulation.

It is the difficulty of paying taxes from the pockets of poverty that makes taxes burdensome, and not their size. If the ability to pay a given amount in tax be tripled, the tax itself may be doubled, and the taxpayers still be the gainers.

Wealth is what labor gets out of the ground; and whatever stimulates labor, or creates a demand for labor, is a direct stimulus to prosperity, by increasing both the number of laborers and the hours of labor, and by affording a market for the products of labor.

If all of those thrown out of positions in a panic were to be put to work by the government in the production of war-materials, there would result no hard times, and the entire country would be better off.

The large standing army indispensable to Germany costs vast sums annually, but the standard of personal efficiency is raised so much by military training, and industry is so stimulated to meet government requirements, that the Germans have captured markets all over the world for the sale of their manufactured products in ever-increasing quantities.

According to statistics, we Americans spend every year on sensuous indulgence, on our hilarities—joy food, joy drink, joy dope, and night-outings—nine thousand million dollars, which, in gold, would weigh more than thirteen thousand tons—the weight of a good-sized battleship.

The biggest super-dreadnoughts cost $15,000,-000 each, built in pairs; built a hundred at a time, they certainly would not cost over $12,000,000 each. We could build, for what we spend on sensuous indulgence, 750 super-dreadnoughts; we could build 160 super-dreadnoughts a year for what we spend on alcoholic beverages; 83 a year for what we spend on tobacco; three a year for what we spend on chewing-gum.

The total amount that we spend each year on our Army and Navy is about $250,000,000. Consequently, we spend more than twelve times as much on alcoholic drinks and tobacco as we do on our Army and Navy.

I do not mean to preach a temperance sermon, or to advise against the use of tobacco. Nevertheless, I do think that for every dollar we spend on indulgence, we might drop a couple of cents into the side-till just for insurance—for the safety of our country against war, in order that our joys of living may be continued.

The small burden of armaments in proportion to the burden of luxuries is very well stated in the following quotation from "Some Economic Aspects of War," by Professor C. Emery:—

"Certainly Bloch is not likely to minimize the extent of such expenditures, as he has been one of the leading writers to show the immensity of this burden, and yet he himself states that the military expenditures of different European countries vary from 2 per cent. to 3.8 per cent. of the total income. Even Germany, with her great organization, takes less than 3 per cent. of the actual income for its maintenance, both of army and navy; and when we think of the expenditures for luxuries, many of them harmful in themselves, the extent of military expenditures appears even less. In Germany, for instance, three times as much is spent for intoxicating drinks as for the support of military and naval establishments. One-third less consumption of beer and liquor on the part of the German people would take care of this part of the budget altogether."

Some Annual United States Expenditures

Sensuous Indulgences, $9,000,000,000 (including alcohol and tobacco)

Alcoholic Drinks, $2,000,000,000

Tobacco, $1,000,000,000

Army and Navy, $250,000,000

Chewing Gum, $36,000,000

There is no branch of insurance so important as insurance against war. There is no other thing insured, of which the loss is so vital as that of one's country, and there is no kind of insurance where the cost of security is so small in comparison with the value of the thing insured. Mr. Stockton puts this very clearly in his book, "Peace Insurance":—

"For insurance against loss by burglary, the nation expends $2,850,000 annually; for insurance against crime in the form of municipal, county, and state police we expend $110,000,000 annually; making a total of $112,850,000 expended for premiums on crime insurance alone. . . . A total annual amount on fire and crime insurance combined is $594,186,104, or about 350 million more than for all our military forces. Considering these figures we may conclude that our military expenditures are by no means greater than the probable loss by a war; that they are small compared with the amounts spent for fire and crime insurance, and that the insurance rate is low compared with that for other kinds of insurance in effect in the business world."

During periods of peace, there tends to be established an equilibrium of supply and demand between our developed industries and our undeveloped resources. Consequently, when war comes and stimulates enormously all our developed industries—arts, sciences, and manufactures—a correspondingly greater demand is placed upon our natural resources, and their development is proportionately increased.

The result is that the nation as a whole is not impoverished in the least by the burden of armaments, but is rather benefited by their support. Also, a nation may likewise be economically benefited by actual war, so long as it has such resources, number of population, industrial arts and sciences, and naval and military equipment as to prevent subjugation and the humiliation and degradation of being forced to pay ransom or tribute in the shape of a large war indemnity to a foreign Power.

The fact that a war indemnity takes gold out of the country, and gives it to another people, makes the indemnity a national calamity. But when money is spent within the country, as it is for armaments, the condition is entirely different.

The following excerpt from "The Valor of Ignorance," by General Homer Lea, admirably presents this:

"Budgets are but the sums total of the symbols of wealth. Whether they are great or small, the wealth of the nation varies not one potato. An individual measures his wealth by coinage, but a nation only by that which coinage represents.

[228]

OUR ARMAMENTS NOT A BURDEN

"As a man squanders his money, he becomes impoverished; but it is only when the resources and means of producing that which money represents are destroyed or diminished that the wealth of a nation is lessened. The armament of a nation, instead of being indicative of its impoverishment, is rather an indication of its capacity."

It is a law of psychology that, when we are subjected to a supreme test, we develop unrealized resources within ourselves; resources that never would be developed, nor could be, except through such trial. By consequence, it is evident that supreme trial is an indispensability to the best development of either individuals or nations. However severe may be the trial that results in the supreme development of the natural resources of the nation, and of the dormant resources in its people, it is essentially beneficial to the nation.

Herbert Spencer said that, just as it is impossible to get a five-fingered hand into a three-fingered glove, with a separate finger in each pocket, so it is impossible to get a complex thought into a mind not sufficiently complex to receive it. It is doubtless impossible, therefore, to prove to the pacifist mind that the money spent in building warships cannot be counted as so much loss to the nation.

The money spent by the government in building fighting-ships could not be esteemed so much money lost, even if the ships were useless. The government taxes the people for the money to build the ships, and then pays the money back to the people again for the ships. The people get their money all back, and the government gets the ships. The people lose nothing, and the government is the gainer to the value of the ships. It may be argued that the labor of the people is lost, but what of it? Labor is neither money nor wealth; it merely represents time. It does not hurt the laborers to do the work; on the contrary, it does them good. They pay but an infinitesimal part of the tax for building the ships. Their occupation constitutes them a market for manufactured articles and farm produce, which pays the manufacturers and the farmers a profit far in excess of their part of the tax for the ships, since by the increased demand they both get better prices and sell more goods. The farmer exerts additional effort to supply the demand, for the laborers who build the ships, and the manufacturers who supply their wares, call upon the farmer for greater supplies of produce than they could call for if the fighting-ships were not built. The farmer, always glad to get more out of the ground when he can sell to advantage, is stimulated to extra effort to get the greater profit, and he is made richer for it. The manufacturer is made richer for it, and the laborer is helped by higher wages and by more continuous occupation.

The result is that the fighting-ships have cost nothing. On the contrary, their production has benefited all. Everybody is made better and richer through the building of them.

It is especially significant and pertinent that the added employment of labor in the construction of armaments adds greatly to the number of tax-payers. Consequently, the burden of taxation is thereby borne by a larger number of persons, with a corresponding lessening of the burden on each individual. This is one of the reasons why poverty is not increased by increased government expenditures in the employment of labor.

The enjoyment of life being derived entirely from exercise of our faculties, the more useful exercise we get within our strength, the happier we are. The building of battleships, by putting us more to use, serves the double purpose of getting more wealth out of the ground and making us happier. It may be argued that this would not be true if our economic institutions were not slack, and that, by perfecting these institutions, every one would receive his due amount of normal stimulus, and would be getting out of the ground his normal amount of wealth. This is all very true, but our economic institutions are not yet perfected, and the cost of building battleships comes out of the slack in our institutions. The work merely helps take up some of the slack.

When we have looked upon our Navy, remembering what the pacifists have told us about its enormous cost, we are strongly impressed with the colossal expenditure, not realizing that the Navy has actually cost nothing. Its production has been a source of profit and benefit to the people.

That which determines the size of a burden is the ability to bear it. Our burden of armaments, borne upon the united backs of a hundred million people, with an aggregate wealth of more than a hundred and thirty billion dollars, with an annual increase of wealth of over four billion dollars, becomes insignificant compared with the ability to support it. Size, like distance and time, has no meaning, except in a relative sense, for space and time are limitless. As compared with space, a mustard seed is exactly as large as the sun.

We hear much about the tremendous burden of the present conflict upon the warring nations. The pacifists tell us that they are destined so to exhaust themselves that, when the war is over, we need have no fear of any one of them, or of a coalition of them, because they will have neither men nor money with which to fight.

The first six months of the war cost about six billion dollars. Now, assuming that the first year of the war should cost even as much as fifteen billion dollars, this would be only five per cent. of the wealth of the warring Powers. But, it must be re-

Enormous Resources of the Warring Nations

Total Wealth of Warring Nations—$300,000,000,000

Total Cost of War for One Year—$15,000,000,000

Total Population of the Warring Nations—500,000,000

Estimated Total Killed and Wounded during first year of present war, based on first six months—4,000,000—less than birth rate by 1,000,000

Estimated Total Killed in one year—800,000—one-sixth the birth rate

membered, that the same thing largely holds true in the case of war that holds true in the case of armaments in time of peace. The cost comes out of the ground, for the most part. In short, the wealth created by the added stimulus in great measure compensates for the loss, especially when the money spent is chiefly returned to the people themselves. The actual out-of-pocket loss to the nations in the present war, taking into account its economic advantages, even during the war, will probably not exceed two and a half per cent., and I doubt if it will amount to that much.

The total number of killed and wounded in the European War during the first six months is estimated at about two million. Most of those wounded will suffer very little permanent injury.

The population of the warring nations is more than four hundred millions, taking into account only such part of the vast Indian population in proportion to the percentage of troops furnished by them as compares with the percentage furnished from the United Kingdom to the number of its inhabitants. Consequently, the total loss in killed and wounded during the first six months of the war was less than a half of one per cent. of the population, and as the number of killed does not exceed ten per cent. of the total number of killed and wounded, the loss during the first six months was about a tenth of half of one per cent.; in other words, only about a twentieth of one per cent.

After the war has run for a year, the total loss in killed and wounded will not exceed one per cent. of the inhabitants, and the total in killed will not exceed a tenth of one per cent.

When the war is over, any one of the warring Powers, unless Germany is exceedingly humbled, will be in better condition in every way to fight us than it would have been before the war broke out.

CHAPTER X

EGO-FANATIC GOOD INTENTIONS AND THEIR RELATION TO NATIONAL DEFENSE

"If you will study history you will find that freedom, when it has been destroyed, has always been destroyed by those who shelter themselves under the cover of its forms, and who speak its language with unparalleled eloquence and vigor."—*Lord Salisbury.*

There is a no more consistent thing in its constancy than human inconsistency.

MANY of those who are most pretentious about the virtue of a meek and lowly spirit manifest characteristics the exact opposite of their self-vaunted pretensions. Often the most enthusiastic and devout workers for a principle are themselves, when put to trial, most pronounced violators of that principle.

Some years ago, while on ship for England, I formed the acquaintance of Sir William Wyndeer, of Australia. He told me that there was a famous woman pacifist on board, who wanted to meet me. She was a notorious militant moral reformer— the Carrie Nation of England. I went with him to where she was sitting on the deck in a steamer-chair, and, on being introduced, sat down beside her.

She opened the conversation with the remark: "Do you know that men like you ought to be hanged; that hanging is too good for you; that men like you, who invent and make explosives and guns to kill people, ought to be killed with them yourselves? That would give you a dose of your own medicine."

I replied by asking her what she thought of the Armenian atrocities, which were at that time being perpetrated.

"What do I think of them?" she answered. "I think just this—that, if I were the Queen of England, I would put an end to that business pretty quick."

"How would you do it?" I asked.

"Why," she responded, "I would go there with an army, and exterminate those beastly Turks."

"If you were to do that," said I, "surely you would need some of the tools for killing people, like those you blame me for inventing, would you not?"—She would not speak to me after that.

In the Dark Ages, they who were responsible for inflicting upon heretics the most exquisite tortures, were the foremost good-intentionists of their time. They believed they were following the teachings of Christ, and applying them in their business and social relations. Their aim was to practise what they preached: "Love one another," "Love thy neighbor as thyself," "On earth peace, good will toward men."

So imbued were they with what they conceived to be divine principles that it was self-evident to them that there was no excuse for any one holding any other opinion than theirs, and that any one who held a different opinion was an enemy of God and man, and should be punished accordingly. They called difference from their opinion heresy, which was branded as the most heinous of all crimes. Those good-intentionists of the Torquemada type racked, flayed, and burned, with a meek and lowly spirit, for the love of God. The horror of St. Bartholomew was to them merely a frolic of brotherly love.

Advocates of disarmament, non-resistance, and the subversion of the military spirit are themselves most militant creatures. They fail to see that, if retiring, non-resistant pacifism is the best policy for a nation to adopt in order to get what it wants, they themselves should adopt such pacifism to get what they want. While they decry every manner of aggression, still they undertake to enforce their doctrines by most aggressive practices.

Never in all human history has any person or class of persons attempted to proselyte others to a doctrine of mildness, meekness, self-sacrifice, and lowly-spiritedness without attempting to enforce the doctrine. In so doing, the practice has been the exact opposite of the preachment.

Robespierre and Marat notably exemplified this truth. Before the French Revolution, Robespierre was noted as a pacifist of the most pretentious cheek-turning type, and Marat was a pacific moralist dyed in the wool. When raised to dictatorial power, however, Robespierre became the wickedest and most venomous of all the fanged monsters of cruelty in the history of mankind; while bloody Marat, clothed with authority, used murder as the sole means of reform. The actions of Robespierre and Marat were the exact opposite of their code for the conduct of others.

The advocates of non-resistance may be perfectly conscientious. It is not to be doubted for one moment that the majority of them are actuated by the best intentions and the kindliest of motives. Torquemada sincerely hoped to do a great good by torturing heretics in the Spanish Inquisition. He is notable among those who have paved broad highways of Hell with good intentions.

The hyper-sentimental pacifists are today actively engaged in paving a broad highway through this country, over which the hell of war is invited by them.

Devotion to the end justified the means to such a well-meaning fanatic as Torquemada. The same was doubtless true of Catherine de' Medici, who mothered the massacre of St. Bartholomew. The

bloody Duke of Alva, Executioner Extraordinary
to Philip II of Spain, who undertook the task of
killing the entire population of the Netherlands,
because their religious opinion differed from the
Spanish brand, could not have been so enthusi-
astically devoted to the monstrous villainy had he
not been inspired by what was to his mind the
best of intentions.

It is remarkable what an influence a very little
thing may sometimes have in shaping the policy
of a people or the fate of a nation. Religious
sects have been formed upon the various interpre-
tations of a single phrase; a difference of opinion
about the meaning of a word has set them at one
another's throats.

Millions upon millions of dollars have been
spent in the United States in peace propagandism,
and eloquent lungs have hoarsed themselves to
defeat Congressional appropriations for defense,
simply because the phrase, *preparation for war,*
has been used instead of the phrase, *preparation
against war.*

An organization of American women, under the
head, Woman's Peace Party, has lately been created. The main resolution adopted by the organization is the following:

"Resolved:
*"That we denounce with all the earnestness of
which we are capable the concerted attempt now*

[239]

being made to force this country into still further preparedness for war. We desire to make a solemn appeal to the higher attributes of our common humanity to help us unmask this menace to our civilization."

They have made the grave mistake of using the expression *for war* in place of the expression *against war*.

The pacifist propagandists, the army and navy men, and all their friends and supporters, are alike agreed that it is wise to make efficient preparations *against* war. None of us wants war, but when we, who believe in armaments, speak of them as preparations *for* war, then the pacifists are in immediate disagreement with us. Let us, therefore, in future substitute the phrase *against war* for the phrase *for war*.

Among the organizers of this so-called party are women of national prominence. They are sincere in their purpose, their aim is high. They are emulating the dictum of Emerson, for they have hitched their wagon to a star—Dr. David Starr—(never mind the Jordan). They solemnly make this pledge:

"We do hereby band ourselves together to demand that war should be abolished."

It is well to note that they have used the word *should* instead of *shall*.

The greatest difficulty in teaching truth is to remove the bias of false learning; for a firm conviction, once established in the mind, gives the mind a fixed set in a certain direction. This is strongly exemplified by the fact that persons who have been proselyted to a certain religious creed can seldom be made to change their faith.

We are what our opinions are. Our opinion shapes our destiny to its own bent. In short, a man is absolutely at the mercy of his opinion.

We have very little to do, however, with the shaping of our own opinion. That is mostly shaped by others. We go to church to have our opinion bent, or its present bent stiffened. We attend a lecture and get a new kink put into our opinion; we converse with our friends, and they dent our opinion; we read books and newspapers, learn something, and are swerved in the direction of our learning, especially in the direction of public opinion. Always and always, while we think that we are shaping our own opinion, we are having it shaped by others.

The estimable ladies of the Woman's Peace Party are merely parading like sandwich men, disporting a legend written on a board by the man higher up, with whom they believe it is most creditable to agree.

At the present time, the false teachings of the peace-propagandists have so proselyted public opinion that every public speaker, aspiring to popular favor, finds it easy, even with a weakling voice and a halting speech, to get his audience with him, and to win a reputation for eloquence and wisdom by prating the bromidial spielings of the peace-propagandists.

A great many men and women in this country hold the same false opinion that the ladies of the Woman's Peace Party hold. Possibly something besides the humiliation of this country by war may lead them into the light of understanding. War, however, will do it, and by their able co-operation with the forces of the future enemies of the country, they are hastening the advent of that war.

If we were to disarm, as these ladies advise, war would come upon us with consternate suddenness. Then, when they saw the desolation and the waste; saw their homes in flames; when they saw innocent citizens clumped in open spaces and shot down with machine-guns; when they saw little children, lean as shadows, starving everywhere; when they encountered insult and maltreatment at every turn; then all their womanhood would revolt and rise up with an altered mind.

Like the light that descended from Heaven on Saul of Tarsus, the light of the truth would descend on those ladies through the smoke of their burning homes—that armed preparedness against such a dread eventuality as war is the supreme of virtue, and its neglect the worst of crimes.

By their help that war is very likely to come, and if it does come, we shall find them, as the women of England, ministering angels in the hospitals of the wounded. We shall find them at the recruiting stations, urging enlistment. We shall find them fitting out their sons, husbands, and brothers for the front. We shall find them, as in England, training in the use of arms as a last emergency reserve. We shall find them, as in England, doing police duty, that the city guardians may go to the front. As the women of Carthage cut the hair from their heads to make bow-strings, so these very women of the Peace Party, as the women of England are doing, as the women of Germany are doing, will sacrifice their jewelry, and all their most precious possessions, to supply the sinews of war.

It is a mistake to suppose that, because men bear arms in war, they are the chief sufferers in war, or make the chief sacrifices. The sexes suffer equally, for to win victory they make mutual and equal sacrifices, and in defeat they suffer mutually every conceivable and every inconceivable laceration of body, pride, and honor.

The supposition is erroneous that woman is less brave or less militant in war than man. In times of peace, when her help is not needed in the sterner affairs of life, she may be as gentle as a dove and as kind as a purring kitten; but, when her help is needed in stern affairs, she is never found wanting. When the cubs are in danger, " the female of the species is more deadly than the male."

The abject condition of Belgian women and children since the German invasion is merely typical of what women and children must inevitably suffer at the hands of invaders. It matters not whether a country be invaded by Germans, Frenchmen, or Englishmen, or by Americans. The stern exigencies of war require that the invaders shall bend every energy and employ every resource to the attainment of the main purpose—victory. The invaders themselves are compelled to make extreme sacrifices, and to bear extreme suffering and privation, and are not in a mood to take on more burden or to suffer extra privations, and, above all, to risk success, in order to alleviate the suffering of the enemy's women and children. Sympathy and mercy, however, do often lead them to be far kinder than would best suit the demands of stern necessity.

It was when Sherman found himself compelled to drive out the civil inhabitants of Atlanta, to prepare for his march to the sea, that in reply to protests on behalf of the women and children, he made his world-famous declaration, "War is hell; and we cannot civilize it or refine it."

The supreme duty of a nation is to safeguard its people from such a crisis and such a calamity. It is useless to lament the miseries of our women and children, after we have, through neglect of national defenses, brought the calamities of war upon them.

With strange inconsistency, the women of the Woman's Peace Party, though they bemoan the lot of the poor women and children of Belgium, are by their own acts inviting the same calamity to fall upon themselves and on their children.

Herbert Spencer observed that individual life is a tendency to establish an equilibrium between internal and external forces. This observation applies also to the life of social organizations, except that, when applied to nations, it should be differently stated, as follows—the life of a nation is the tendency to establish an equilibrium between internal forces, and also between those forces and external forces.

Opposing forces separately tend toward instability of equilibrium, but collectively, by operating against one another, they tend to the establishment of an equilibrium. Individual action in a group of individuals tends to heterogeneity, aggregated action to homogeneity. One of the mainsprings of progress is the pertinacity of enthusiasts and faddists. Even the self-appointed ego-fanatic moral reformers are often useful, because they tend to throw society out of balance. This rouses the great mass of the people to inquiry and raises them to a broader understanding, with the result that, in the end, pernicious propagandists, who have overshot the mark, are brought back nearer the mark, and the sane mass of the people brought nearer the mark. A fanatic reformer sometimes injects dynamic force into a static condition. It seems to be a rational assumption, therefore, that, in all things where organized feminist fanaticism of both men and women is today working evil, the great body of sane and normal men and women ought to exert their united influence to the full as a stabilizer, or equilibrator of the social organization.

CHAPTER XI

A DANGEROUS CRIMINAL CLASS?

"Probably the most curious feature of the naval program is the regularity with which the sky clouds over as the day for the consideration of naval appropriations approaches. Year after year, after a long spell of pleasant weather, all at once storm clouds have drifted across the heavens, international relations have become suddenly strained, and the whole land has lain in the shadow of an impending conflict. Fortunately, the storm blows over as soon as the votes are counted, and in the beautiful sunlight which follows the storm, workmen are seen constructing additional battleships. Suspicious persons have occasionally imagined they saw a connection between the international weather and the Navy League."

Dr. Charles E. Jefferson.

"It is criminal that we should expend vast sums on warships and armament on the advice of interested parties alone. . . ."

"War scares are heard the world over. The world over they are set going by wicked men for evil purposes."

Dr. David Starr Jordan, "War and Waste."

THE pacifists have delved out of the infinite latency a very startling alleged truth, which they are effulging in language of lavish luminosity, to the effect that it is necessary only for a man to have a pecuniary interest or personal advantage involved in order to commit any kind of crime. They have discovered that room for a motive establishes the motive and proves the crime. They have discovered that those things which we call integrity and honor and conscience are no deterrents whatsoever to the commission of the most heinous offense against one's fellow men, so long as there is profit in it. They believe that, if only there is money in the game, an inventor or manufacturer or merchant will scheme for the commission of wholesale poisoning, maiming, and murder. They believe that the inventors and manufacturers of guns necessarily foster war in order to promote the sale of their wares. They surmise that inventors and manufacturers of smokeless powders and high explosives are capable of standing with the "black hand," capable of being gladdened at the dynamite outrage, at the street riot, at the slaughter of song-birds—anything that will consume dynamite or burn gunpowder.

According to the pacifists, the principal lay of makers of war-materials is to connive with the officers of the Army and Navy to stir up international dissension and foment war, in order to create a demand for their products. The pacifists believe that army and navy officers are only too willing to co-operate in the nefarious business, because war brings higher pay and rapid promotion. They believe that it matters not to these "interested parties" how many of their countrymen are sacrificed on the firing line, or how many widows and orphans are made. The groans of the wounded and dying on the battle-field, and the lamentations in the desolated home, are music to the ears of those who supply the war-materials; for, with every shot from a rifle, fifty grains of gunpowder are burned, while bullets enough miss their mark to equal the weight of each man they kill. Consequently, there is substantial profit to the cartridge-maker and the gunpowder-manufacturer for every man killed with a rifle ball.

But it is in shrapnel and the ammunition for the big guns that the greatest profit lies. Field-guns fire away ammunition costing from ten to twenty dollars a shot, at the rate of from twenty to forty shots a minute. This costs a lot of money. At the battle of Mukden, in the Russo-Japanese war, one battery of eight guns fired 11,159 rounds, or 1,395 rounds per gun. Think of the expense of that ammunition, and the profit to the manufacturers! It is estimated that when the big naval guns are fired, the cost of the smokeless-powder charge, the projectile and bursting charge, together with the wear and tear of the gun, amounts to more than $2,000 a shot, and the damage done to a warship hit may be many millions.

Look at it any way you will, war, according to the pacifist notion, is a real Klondike for manufacturers of war-materials. The peace sophists have been able to put two and two together, with the conclusions that such an opportunity for profit is too strong for human nature to resist, and that, as they have found room for the motive, they have proved the crime.

Of course, their accusation is a pretty severe arraignment of human nature, after all these years of civilization and Christian enlightenment.

It is strange how human nature can have improved so much lately, as claimed by the pacifists, and how the spirit of brotherhood and good-will can have suddenly become so dominant that the peoples of the earth now despise war, and are so afflicted with the horrors of it that, just as soon as the great European War is over, they are not going to fight any more, while still the makers of war-materials remain in the primitive savagery of the stone age. It seems to me that, if human nature has so improved as to be an efficient bar to a nation against waging war for plunder, regardless of the advantage and the profit, it ought also to be a similar bar to inventors and manufacturers of war-materials, and to army and navy officers, against precipitating war for pecuniary or personal advantage.

But, according to pacifist reasoning, those ''interested parties'' are more endowed with the spirit of the hyena than with the spirit of brotherhood. Perhaps, however, the manufacturers of war-materials, and army and navy officers, were not home when the great improvement in human nature knocked at their door.

If considerations of mere personal profit are sufficient to make the best of us foster war, which the peace fanatics esteem wholesale murder, it is strange that the inventors and manufacturers of drugs and medicines, the proprietors of drug-stores, and the medical profession and under-takers, do not form a league and co-operate in spreading infectious diseases, in order to create a greater demand for their wares and for their services.

Of course, the reason may be that they have not yet thought of it, and it may be wrong for me to suggest the thing to them. Still, it is queer that it has not been suggested to them by what the pacifists have said concerning the conduct of our army and navy officers and of the inventors and manufacturers of war-materials.

Let us see what the facts actually are:

The inventors and manufacturers of war-materials, and our army and navy officers, by virtue of the study and experience that qualify them for their business or profession better than others, are also qualified better than others to judge what are our actual needs for national defense.

If the manufacturers of war-materials, and our army and navy men, are to be convicted of inciting war on the evidence that by so doing they create a demand for their services, then necessarily others benefited by a like demand may be convicted on the same evidence.

[251]

Mr. Andrew Carnegie himself is the greatest of all American armorers. He it was who introduced the Bessemer steel process into the United States, from which all our gun-makers and all our armament-makers have greatly benefited. It is his name and that of Herr Krupp which Neptune reads graven in the walls of fighting-ships. He still draws an income from his interests in the great armor-making steel corporation—an annual income big enough to pay the combined salaries of all the four thousand officers of the United States Army.

Truly, if the discovery of room for a motive proves both the motive and the crime, and is sufficient to convict these four thousand men of being willing to sell their souls in order to raise their salaries a few dollars, Mr. Carnegie himself is at least open to suspicion.

Likewise, the varied and many institutions—incubators of the doves of peace—born of the great armor-maker's generosity, which continue to be his beneficiaries, cannot escape the suspicion that taints their pedigree.

Even the leading man—the principal star on the stage where *Uncle Sammy unter Alles* is being played—Dr. David Starr Jordan, is paid from the Carnegie Peace Foundation with money equally tainted by the sweaty hands of the grimy men who are forging armor-plate in the Smoky City.

But we all know that Mr. Carnegie is above any

such suspicion. We know that the pacifist method of reasoning must be false.

The education of our army and navy officers teaches them not alone military science, but also national devotion and personal honor. Devotion to duty is necessary in order to keep them in the service, under the altogether inadequate pay they receive. The pay of the American army and navy officers is smaller, in proportion to their knowledge and the value of their services, than that of any other class of men in the country. If every army and navy officer should abandon the service for a position in civil life when he could get a raise of wages for so doing, there would not be a corporal's guard left in the service.

Whenever a public work is placed in charge of an army or navy officer, there is no *sub-rosa* rake-off, or divvy with civilian contractors. There is absolutely no graft of any kind in their service, and the government is sure of getting the maximum amount of work for the minimum cost. Not one cent of graft has fallen upon the palms either of Colonel Goethals or of any other army officer in the whole course of construction of that mighty work—the Panama Canal. New York City tried to get Colonel Goethals as Police Commissioner. He has received scores of offers of positions in civil life at many times his present salary, because of the military capacity and honor that make the Goethals sort of service very valuable.

I know many army and navy men intimately. I have had opportunities of hearing their off-guard conversations and interchange of ideas on all manner of subjects, and have thereby been enabled to see their character revealed to the naked soul, and I have never yet discovered any other attitude or tendency among them than the emulation of exactly that type of honor, efficiency, and manhood which is Colonel Goethals'.

I cannot award this same high praise to the politicians I have known.

An army or navy officer always drives just as close a bargain as he can on behalf of the government when doing business with civilians, although the economics of the transaction is of no personal concern to him.

When a politician makes a bargain, his first consideration is: "Where do I come in?" His next consideration is: "Where does the party come in?" Duty to the government is a minor consideration.

It is the demand for a thing that leads to its invention, just as it is the demand for a thing that leads to its manufacture. The demand must precede the production.

When the inventor designs a gun, or invents a new explosive, he does not simultaneously try to invent ways and means of creating a market. He may, on the contrary, be inspired with a spirit of patriotism, and feel that in the event of war his work will be of signal service to his country, both by killing his country's enemies and by saving the lives of his own people.

The manufacturers of war-materials are much more likely to be actuated by honorable motives, and to make large sacrifices from a spirit of patriotism, than are the manufacturers of soap, agricultural machinery, or automobiles.

The builders of Ericsson's *Monitor* were not able to get the government either to approve or to back the enterprise. They were, however, fortunately inspired by a high spirit of patriotism, and by a strong belief in Ericsson's invention; consequently, they built it at their own expense. It was completed just in the nick of time. The terrible *Merrimac* appeared before the *Monitor* was quite ready. She could laugh at forts, and the projectiles from the guns of our wooden navy glanced off her mailed sides like raindrops off a duck's back. Whether she would be able to run up the Potomac and bombard Washington, was a question only of the depth of water.

The little coterie of bureaucrats in Washington, who had ridiculed the fantastic innovation of Ericsson, were now on Uneasy Street, and sent urgent appeals for the *Monitor* to be made ready and sent to Hampton Roads with all speed. The peculiar craft did arrive on the morning of the second day of the naval fight. The result is one of the good stories of history—a story that has never been quite equaled in fiction.

The *Monitor* had not yet been accepted by the government when she fought the *Merrimac;* she had not yet received the government's approval.

A country Reuben, who saw a giraffe for the first time at a circus, looked the animal over, and, finding that it did not conform to his ideas of what an animal ought to be, remarked, "By gum, there ain't no sich critter!" Likewise, the naval experts at Washington did not believe that there could be any such fighting-ship. After that fight, however, the *Monitor* was quickly purchased, and hurried orders were given for more *Monitors.*

The patriotism and pluck of the warship-builders saved the country.

The pacifists are strongly urging what they term the nationalization of all manufacture of war-materials; that is to say, that all such materials should be made at government plants. Their object is to have the work done by disinterested persons, who will not be tempted to promote war in order to make a market for those materials. By admirable inconsistency, the pacifists would, in so doing, place the manufacture of war-materials in the hands of army and navy officers, whom they pronounce the most pernicious of all promoters of war.

Before Congress acts upon the suggestion of

the pacifists to nationalize the manufacture of all war-materials, it would be well to see what would have happened in the past, had the thing been done sooner. We can judge from that concerning the advisability of adopting the measure now.

If it had been adopted at the time of the Civil War, Ericsson's *Monitor* never would have been built, because its building depended upon private personal patriotism and private enterprise.

If the measure had been adopted twenty-five years ago, then naturally, during that period, private invention and private enterprise would have been eliminated, and the government would not have profited from civilian genius and energy. Let us see, then, what private invention and private enterprise have done for the government for the past quarter-century, since the advent of smokeless powder.

Colonel E. G. Buckner, vice-president of the du Pont Powder Company, in an article in *Harper's Weekly,* of June 27, 1914, places the credit for the four most important inventions in the development of smokeless powder—first, to Vieille, of France, who produced gun-cotton; second, to Mendeléeff, of Russia, who told us how to colloid it; third, to Francis G. du Pont, who eliminated danger in the manufacture; and, fourth, to Hudson Maxim, who invented the multi-perforated grain that gave absolute control over the burning.

It will be seen that two of the most important steps in the development of smokeless powder were made by American civilian inventors. The alcohol replacement invention of Francis G. du Pont and my own invention of the multi-perforated grain, rendered possible the use of a colloid of pure nitro-cellulose as a smokeless cannon-powder. It would be absolutely impossible successfully to make a pure nitro-cellulose cannon-powder without these two inventions. If the manufacture of smokeless powder had been nationalized twenty-five years ago, this government would not stand, as it stands today, ahead of all other governments, in the excellence of its smokeless powder.

When the government first ordered a pure nitro-cellulose powder, large quantities of solvents were consumed in its preparation. Private manufacturers introduced new processes to overcome this difficulty, resulting in a material reduction in the cost of the powder, which has already effected a saving to the government of more than $2,000,000.

It is a peculiarity of smokeless powder that, regardless of however stable it may be when first made, it gradually begins to decompose after long standing, which, until recently, necessitated its destruction. Several years ago, however, Mr. Francis I. du Pont, son of the Francis G. du Pont above-mentioned, invented a process for the successful reworking of smokeless powder that has begun to decompose, at a mere fraction of the original cost, making it just as good as ever. This invention alone will hereafter save the government more than a million dollars a year.

When the new army rifle was developed, it was found that the smokeless powder then used by the army, containing nitro-glycerin, was so erosive as to destroy the accuracy of the arm when only 1,600 rounds had been fired. The government obtained from abroad some smokeless powder, which enabled 3,000 rounds to be fired before the gun was destroyed, but after that number of rounds, the rifling was practically obliterated.

A private manufacturer invented a new smokeless rifle-powder, with process and apparatus for its manufacture. With this powder, it is now possible to fire as high as 20,000 rounds before the accuracy of the gun is destroyed. This invention easily multiplies the life of the army rifle by six. As the army rifle will now last six times as long by the use of this powder as it would by the use of any other powder, the value of the invention to the government is by far the chief value of the gun itself. Consequently, it is estimated that this invention alone represents a value for the guns that the government now has on hand of more than $15,000,000.

Not only does our small-arms powder effect a great saving in the wear and tear of our shoulder-rifles, but also our pure nitro-cellulose cannon-powder effects a similar saving in the life of our big guns. Our big guns, using pure nitro-cellulose powder, last, with equal accuracy, more than twice as long as British guns, which use cordite.

It will be seen from the foregoing considerations and figures that private genius and private enterprise alone have saved the government very many millions of dollars. Of course, it may be argued that, since guns and ammunition and all kinds of military implements and engines have been perfected, there is not now room for civilian inventors to be so useful to the government during the next twenty-five years as they have been in the past twenty-five.

A similar attitude of the average mind would have existed had the same question been raised twenty-five years ago. When our Patent Office was first established, the Commissioner of Patents predicted that within fifty years everything possible of invention would have been invented and that then the Patent Office would have to be abolished for lack of business. The number of inventions received by the Patent Office, however, has rapidly increased, and is still rapidly increasing. More inventions are received now each year at the Patent Office than were received during the first fifty years of its existence. The reason for this is that every invention, either directly or indirectly, creates a demand for other inventions.

The inventor is still working in virgin soil, and the room for invention is infinite.

If the manufacture of war-materials were to be nationalized, not only would the government rob itself of the aid of large quasi-government manufactories, but also it would rob itself of the benefits of the inventive genius of the whole people. The value of that genius may be approximated by recalling what citizen inventions have done since the outbreak of the American Civil War.

Breech-loading guns of all kinds, the percussion cap, cartridges for small-arms, fixed ammunition for quick-firing guns, the breech mechanism for all guns, the built-up gun, the great improvements in steel manufacture, the revolving turret and the *Monitor* type of fighting-ship, the steam turbine, the internal-combustion engine, all of the great inventions in smokeless powders and high explosives, and their adaptability to use in ordnance, the submarine torpedo-boat, the self-propelled torpedo, the aëroplane and the dirigible, and any number of other inventions indispensable to modern warfare, have been the invention of civilians. Of course, army and navy officers have invented a great many important things themselves, and have rendered great service in the development of civilian inventions. But it must be remembered that army and navy officers constitute but a very small part of the population. Even were army and navy men ten times more proficient in the invention of war-materials than civilian inventors, the number and value of civilian naval and military inventions would preponderate enormously over those of government officers.

We have been assured all along by the peace sophists that, if war should come, the great American genius would rise to the occasion and spring to our rescue, with all manner of destructive contrivances, capable of annihilating armies and sweeping fleets of fighting-ships off the seas.

If the beautiful nationalization plan of the peace sophists, however, were to be carried out, the great American genius would get no opportunity to fructify the prophesied militant cataclysmic ogerism to the discomfiture of our enemies.

No other government has nationalized the manufacture of armaments and war-materials to the exclusion of private manufacturers. On the contrary, other governments strongly encourage private manufacture, for they realize the vast importance of drawing upon the inventive genius of the whole people, and of enlisting private energy, private enterprise, and private capital in government work.

The French government for more than a hundred years has made all its own gunpowder, but its chief gun-works are private enterprises. Possibly, if the French smokeless powder had been perfected by private enterprise to meet government requirements, those requirements would have been more exacting with private manufacturers than with government manufacturers, and the battleships *Jéna* and *La Liberté* would not have been blown up by the spontaneous combustion of bad gunpowder. If this government were to nationalize the manufacture of its war-materials, we know, by what has been done in the past, through private enterprise and private inventive genius, that the government would suffer enormously.

In this era of Congressional investigations, it would be well to have a government inquiry made as to whether or not there should be a new classification of acts of treason. It should be inquired whether or not, in time of peace, public preachments should be allowed advocating the disbanding of our Army and the destruction of our Navy —acts which in time of war might be interpreted as treason, and the offenders backed up against a wall and shot. It should be inquired whether or not foreign emissaries, and possibly spies, have not for years been collaborating with American advocates of disarmament. It should be inquired whether or not the Washington lobby that has been operating against governmental appropriations for the Army and Navy, has not received foreign support. If these things have not been done by representatives of foreign countries, with such a wide-open opportunity, then the diplomats and strategists of foreign nations ought to be sent to a kindergarten for instruction. Could anything be more likely than that foreign Powers should possess the sagacity to grasp such an opportunity to weaken our defenses?

CHAPTER XII

THE GOOD AND EVIL OF PEACE AND OF WAR

" All states are in perpetual war with all. For that which we call peace is no more than merely a name, whilst in reality Nature has set all communities in an unproclaimed but everlasting war against each other."   *Plato.*

SO much has been said based on ignorance and false premise about the good and evil of war, and the good and evil of peace, that a few cold, relevant facts will not be out of place here.

In stating these facts, the writer is standing neither as sponsor for war nor as sponsor for peace. He is not posing as a judge qualified to pass sentence on peace or on war, but merely as one who understands the subject sufficiently to throw some new light upon it. In bearing witness to the cruelty and mercilessness of Nature, the writer assumes no responsibility for what Nature has done; he was not consulted. In bearing witness to the evils and benefits of war, and the evils and benefits of peace, the writer does not thereby either palliate the evils, or stand responsible for them; neither does he assume credit for their benefits and blessings. He realizes, however, that the bearer of bad tidings is associated with the ill-feeling they inspire, although he may be wholly innocent of the ill.

While too much stress cannot be laid upon the horrors of war and the individual suffering incurred thereby, still it is not just to lay to the account of war or militarism every ill that flesh is heir to, as is done by many of the pacifi-maniacs. As a matter of fact, it would be as justifiable to attack peace because of the evils that develop in times of peace. We do not, however, on that account conceive peace to be a misfortune, but a blessing.

While our pacifists promote war by their teachings, they declaim against war and picture its horrors and calamitous results. One would naturally suppose that, appreciating what a terrible thing war is, they would take the most scientific and dependable means of safeguarding this country against such a calamity; but, as a matter of fact, they are doing everything in their power to abolish the one means that can safeguard us against war. With consistent inconsistency, they place the blame for war on the advocates of adequate armaments—the true peace-advocates and peace-makers and enemies of war, who are forefending us against war. The advocacy of armaments is construed by them as the advocacy of war; measures for peace are confounded with measures for breaching the peace.

A curious phase of the matter is that many friends of armaments themselves make a similar mistake, and think that in defending armaments they are called upon to defend war also. As a matter of fact, war has no defense, except as a last resort. But when there is no other way, and when the maintenance of peace would be a greater calamity than war, then war is to be recommended as the lesser evil. It is, nevertheless, undeniably an evil, though a necessary one, just as a surgical operation is a necessary evil—but one which, if successful, results in such good as far to outweigh the evil.

The peace sophists tell us that there has never been a good war or a bad peace; that always in war the best specimens of manhood have been slain, leaving the weak and unfit for breeding purposes. They tell us that the Napoleonic wars lowered the stature of the entire French nation by two inches. They tell us also that during all past ages war for plunder has been the principal business of mankind.

The following arraignment of war by General Hiram M. Chittenden is a very fair sample of this method of reasoning:

"Both in its restriction upon marriage and in its destruction of life war thus destroys the most

precious seed and leaves the inferior from which to propagate. In proportion as wars are long continued, and draw heavily upon the population, these deleterious effects are apparent. The campaigns of Napoleon were a mighty drain upon the vigor of the French people. It has been held that the average stature of the French was thereby diminished by more than an inch. How much their intellectual and moral stature was shrunken by that debauchery of crime, who can say? The decadence of the Roman people was due more to the waste of its best blood in war than to the causes commonly accepted. War reverses the process of natural selection and, instead of producing the survival of the fittest, produces the survival of the most unfit."

According to statistics of the pacifists, from the year 1496 B.C. to the year 1861 A.D.—a period of 3,357 years—there were 227 years of peace and 3,130 years of war—thirteen years of war for every year of peace. Now, if what we are told about the degenerative effects of war is true, since we know that war has been prevalent in all ages, the natural conclusion is, what a lot of rapscallions we must be! If war, instead of tending to secure the survival of the fit, secures the survival of the unfit, then after a thousand centuries of strife we must be signally unfit.

The trouble with such statistics is that, instead

[268]

of leading us toward the truth, they lead us into error. It may be perfectly true that for every year of general peace there have been thirteen years when there was a war somewhere on the earth; but this does not imply in the least that peace was not more general than was war, even during those thirteen years when there was a war. We must remember that the history of nations does not tell us much about the affairs of the people in times of peace; it is their wars that have made history.

As we look back through time at the large number of wars, we clump them together in perspective. We place the wars, as it were, all on the map at once, instead of placing them years and centuries apart.

Just as there is always in human life more joy than sorrow, more pleasure than pain, more good than ill; so, in the history of the world, there has been more of peace and prosperity than there has been of war and calamity.

John Ruskin possessed the rare ability to perceive truth that pointed one way, while his feelings pointed in the opposite direction. Although he had an emotional nature and a highly artistic temperament, he was still a man of so broad views, with so comprehensive a mind at the other end of the optic nerve, that he could ratiocinate in spite of his emotions. The following is what he had to say on war:

[269]

"All the pure and noble arts of peace are founded on war; no great art ever rose on earth but among a nation of soldiers. There is no great art possible to a nation but that which is based on battle. When I tell you that war is the foundation of all the arts, I mean also that it is the foundation of all the high virtues and faculties of men. It was very strange for me to discover this, and very dreadful, but I saw it to be quite an undeniable fact. The common notion that peace and the virtues of civil life flourished together I found to be utterly untenable. Peace and the vices of civil life only flourish together. We talk of peace and learning, of peace and plenty, of peace and civilization; but I found that these are not the words that the Muse of History coupled together: that on her lips the words were peace and sensuality, peace and selfishness, peace and death. I found in brief that all great nations learned their truth of word and strength of thought in war; that they were nourished in war and wasted in peace; taught by war and deceived by peace; trained by war and betrayed by peace; in a word, that they were born in war and expired in peace."

We must not conclude, from the above quotation from Ruskin, that he was an advocate of brutality versus humanity, for he was not. The thought he meant to convey was simply this—that only a supreme trial, a supreme responsibility, where country, life itself, and that which is dearer than life—home—are staked on the issue, can bring out the highest virtues. The struggle for inalienable human rights, whose observance is freedom, has been the greatest influence to stimulate the genius and the virtues of men, and these things have been accomplished, and could only have been accomplished, by war.

The humanity of Ruskin is well brought out in the following quotation:

" . . . *Depend upon it, all work must be done at last, not in a disorderly, scrambling, doggish way, but in an ordered, soldierly, human way—a lawful or 'loyal' way. Men are enlisted for the labor that kills—the labor of war: they are counted, trained, fed, dressed, and praised for that. Teach the plough exercise as carefully as you do the sword exercise, and let the officers of troops of life be held as much gentlemen as the officers of troops of death; and all is done: but neither this, nor any other right thing, can be accomplished— you can't even see your way to it—unless, first of all, both servant and master are resolved that, come what will of it, they will do each other justice.*"

Ralph Waldo Emerson held the same opinion about war as that held by John Ruskin. He quoted and approved the old Greek, Heraclitus, who said, "War is the father of all things." After quoting this expression, Emerson said, "We of this day can repeat it as a political and social truth." Also, he said, "War passes the power of all chemical solvents, breaking up the old cohesions, and allowing the atoms of society to take a new order."

As a matter of fact, social order, in time of peace, like a cultivated field, settles and solidifies, and it must be broken down into subsoil, to support a new and vigorous growth. The breaking by plough and dynamite, uprooting and submerging all undesirable growth, is rewarded by healthy and vigorous crops of a desirable growth.

The very privations that have to be endured by large numbers of persons during a great war, stimulate economy, invention, and extraordinary endeavor, and serve to teach many useful lessons and to impart valuable experiential knowledge, which is applied both during the war, and, with greater advantage, when the war is over. When a country is at war, all its industries are not rendered stagnant or idle, but many of them are stimulated to extraordinary effort when cut off from import by blockade.

The legend about the stature of the French nation being lowered two inches as a result of killing off so many of the best men of France during the Napoleonic wars, is a very plausible one,

and one that has been made great use of by the
pacifists. But no one has thought to inquire
whether or not, during the past century, the average stature of the Spaniards and the Italians also
has been lowered. Perhaps, if we should inquire,
we might learn that the color of the hair and eyes
and skin of the French had somewhat darkened
during that period. We might learn the truth
that the effect upon the stature and the color of
the eyes and skin and hair was mainly due to another kind of warfare—that of the southern blood
of the Latin against the blood of the blond Norse-
man. We might learn that in Italy, Spain, and
France, the posterity of the Norse giants, who
long ago overran and conquered those countries,
did not thrive well there, but slowly died down.
We might learn that in those lands the blood of
the blond is gradually overcome by the blood of
the brunette; and that, as the blond races are
larger in stature, the stature of the mixed Latin
races is lowered in proportion to the disappear-
ance of the blond type. The ancient Roman was
much shorter in stature than even the present
Italian or Frenchman.

Warfare has always subjected the weak, the
puny, the poor, the ill, the indigent, and the incompetent to privations, trials, and strains of such
severity that they have died in large numbers.
They have not been so able as normal persons to
escape the sword and to resist famine and disease;

consequently, fewer of them have survived than of the more fit.

It is, however, argued by the peace sophists, that in modern warfare only the most able-bodied men are selected for military duty, and also that the weak and unfit who remain at home are not subjected to the same exterminating influences as formerly.

As a matter of fact, comparing the results of war today with those in former years, we find the percentage of deaths among the incompetent stay-at-homes far larger than among the soldiers at the front.

It is true that medical science secures the survival of a much larger percentage of stay-at-home incompetents than in former years, but medical science saves also a much larger proportion of those injured in battle than formerly, so that the ratio of survival between the fit and the incompetent is today in favor of the fit. The conditions that tend to secure the survival of the fittest are even more effective today than they were in old-time wars.

The unpleasant truth should be realized that invading armies must, with other luxuries, have women. As a result, they leave a large progeny— wrens in the nests of the doves of peace. Hence, inasmuch as soldiers are the pick of the manhood of their country, they are likely to do about as much toward securing the survival of the fit in an enemy's country as they would have in their own country.

There is another very important consideration, which is that war is a great mixer of races, and that usually mixed types benefit enormously from their compound blood.

Furthermore, the mingling of races and peoples has in all times served greatly to spread knowledge of one another, and they have always profited largely from the mingled knowledge. Soldiers visiting distant lands have brought home acquaintance with new arts and sciences and broader ideas of international usefulness. The soldiers of the North, who marched with Sherman through Georgia to the sea, returned years afterward and built cotton mills, iron foundries, and machine-shops all over the South, and stimulated the South with Northern energy and Northern capital.

We know that the inhabitants of the earth are constantly growing more fit; consequently, we know that they cannot be growing constantly more unfit, due to the degenerative influence of war. The history of nations is a history of wars; consequently we know as untrue the contention of the peace sophists that war secures the survival of the unfit. We know that exactly the opposite must be true; that war secures the survival of the fit.

There is yet another thing of which the peace sophists have never thought, and could not be expected to think—the tremendous self-saving potentiality of the race.

As I have pointed out elsewhere, Nature seems to care little for individuals, but everything for a race or species; consequently, Nature has fore-fended herself by very ample measures to insure the survival of the fit.

If every able-bodied man in the world today were to be slain, and only the weak and puny left, although the injury would be incalculable and would make the whole race stagger, still the next generation of men would be almost as able-bodied and as fit as the present generation. Let us see why: It is because of that great potentiality—atavism. Children inherit not only directly from their parents, but their inheritance harks back to grandfather, great-grandfather, and even to re-mote ancestry.

Just as a stream of water burdened with im-purities is self-purifying when it suns itself on the bright pebbles and on grass and moss that web and tangle it, so life is self-purifying and self-regen-erative. Nature is constantly reaching higher and higher. The acquired characteristics of parents tend to become instinctive in their children. In-stinct is largely inherited experience.

Nature strives to protect herself against degen-eracy. Though bad conduct on the part of parents harmfully affects the child, yet such influences are less potent than those that are regenerative. If this were not true, Nature's ends would not be so well secured.

There is in all animal organisms a certain innate power of resistance to germs of disease, and there is likewise in man a similar power of resistance to degeneracy.

The forces that operate to protect the individual operate also to shield the species by affording protection against evil inheritance.

Abnormal types are not always representative of diseased or degenerate conditions; other considerations must be weighed. Even some criminals may be atavic examples of a class of individuals who were better suited to live under the savage conditions that existed many generations ago.

Nature has resources for her protection far beyond our ken. Some of them have, by our inquiry, been discovered. We have discovered that not only do we immunize ourselves to withstand repeated attacks from the same disease, but also our children to some extent inherit that immunity.

When syphilis, the most abominable disease that ever afflicted mankind, was brought to Europe by the sailors of Columbus, the Europeans, possessing no immunity against it, died by hundreds of thousands. It afflicted equally all classes, from peasant to king. This disease among the West Indian tribes was slow-moving, and comparatively mild; but it became exceedingly virulent, rapid, and almost always fatal, in the blood of the un-immunized people of the Old World. This disease alone has been more harmful to the human race than all the wars of the world since the dawn of human history.

Although today the Old-World races have acquired considerable immunity to that affliction and although science has discovered a rational and comparatively successful treatment, it is still the greatest single degenerative influence with which the race has to contend. Its evil potency is greatly enhanced by the facility with which it weds alcoholism, and breeds tuberculosis, cancer, and paranoia.

The old pioneers sowed the western continent and the islands of the sea with the germs of smallpox and measles. Smallpox, terrible anywhere, was tenfold more so with the newly discovered peoples. Measles was more fatal with the Indians than smallpox with the Europeans. Only recently, in Alaska, whole communities have been wiped out by the measles. Even chicken-pox, harmless with us, was nearly always fatal to the inhabitants of the Pacific Islands.

The races, however, gradually but surely, developed immunity, and the great world-scourges are now largely robbed of their terrors. Similarly has mankind developed powers of recuperation that largely tend to immunization against such degenerative effects as are of war.

When a large limb is lopped from a tree, the mother-stem puts out a new shoot, and grows another strong limb in its place; similarly, when limbs are lopped from the human family tree, new limbs are stimulated to growth. This peculiarity of living things is strangely manifested in certain species, particularly among the lower orders of animals. Certain animals have no way of seeking self-preservation except by breeding in such large numbers as to supply the appetites of all enemies, and glut the demand. A big salmon sometimes lays a gallon of small eggs, often numbering as high as 27,000,000. Certain species of polyp are provided no means whatever, either by speed or powers of resistance, to defend themselves, but they breed so rapidly that they cannot all be eaten.

Now that we have defended war against the charge of securing the survival of the unfit, and have proved that, on the contrary, war has, during all the ages, been instrumental in securing the survival of the fit, let us, without presuming against peace, see whether or not peace has a blameless record.

The long periods of peace during the past century have allowed the peoples time and opportunity to acquire wealth and luxury, and to develop peculiar tastes, especially along emotional lines. . . . Modern fiction is a universal love story. Art is largely a portrayal of sentimentality.

In olden times, when human suffering in every guise, born of war, was very common, the appeals of the poor, the weak, and the infirm were not much heeded, for there were ever present such severe and exacting concerns as to command the attention and to absorb the resources of the people.

In time of peace less rigid economy is practised than in time of war. Dangers and hardships, which are the concomitants of war, have been found in all ages better formative influences for making hardy, successful men than a life of ease, comfort, and luxury. Consequently, in time of peace there is a far more preponderant tendency toward degeneracy and national decay than there is in time of war, in spite of the large numbers of fine specimens of manhood that are killed in war.

When Cyrus the Great, with his hardy mountaineers, had conquered the peace-loving, comfort-loving people of the lowlands, he told his soldiers that they must not make their homes in the lowlands, but must return to their mountain fastnesses, because if they settled to a life of ease and luxury, they would become unwarlike, effeminate, and degenerate, like the lowlanders they had conquered and enslaved, and later would themselves be conquered and enslaved by other mountaineers inured to privations and hardships, who would descend upon them.

Witness the wisdom of Herodotus, who said:

"It is the settled appointment of Nature that soft soils should breed soft men, and that the same land should never be famous for the excellence of its fruit and for the vigor of its inhabitants."

Montesquieu said:

"The barrenness of the soil makes men industrious, sober, hard-working, courageous, and warlike, for they must obtain by their own exertion that which the earth denies them, whilst the fertility of a country produces in them love of ease, indolence, and a sense of cautious self-preservation."

The ancient Spartans in time of peace voluntarily subjected themselves to every privation and hardship necessary to keep them in prime condition for instant war.

Nature is never moved by pity. Nature is not a sentimentalist. The earthquake shock is no respecter of persons. When a ship founders, the angry waves of the sea show no mercy to the drowning, and have no pity for those struggling to survive in the life-boats. The arctic airs of winter are as savage to those exposed to them as

are the teeth of wolves. All animal life on the
earth must constantly contend with both the devouring elements of Nature and the devouring
greed of other animal life.

Pity is a child of the imagination, and is, for
that reason, a peculiarly human attribute. It
is a very noble trait, and is of material aid in
greatening mutual human usefulness. Nevertheless, no one thinks for a moment of blaming any
of the lower animals for their appetites and passions; they are understood to be normal and necessary. Similarly, all our normal appetites and
passions are necessary. Considered in the broad,
as natural attributes, there are no such things as
bad normal emotions and passions; it is only when
they become perverted by degeneracy or abuse
that they are evil.

The passion of pity may be perverted and
abused just as the sex appetite or the appetite
for food and drink.

If human pity had dominated the council at the
creation of the world, the result would have been
infinite injury, because none of the higher orders
of animals, even man himself, could have been
developed. In short, there would have been no intelligent beings on earth.

During periods of peace, a large number of persons, moved by pity for the indigent, the halt, the
lame, the blind, extend to them the alleviating hand
of charity. Philanthropy finds favor in the public

eye, and charity becomes a cheap and easy means
of courting public opinion. The philanthropist
with means for gratifying his passion of pity, or
the ambitious aspirant for public favor with cash
to invest in public opinion, finds himself soon surrounded with a multitude of itchy-palmy hands to
help him spend his money to buy what he is after,
and at the same time obtain profit for themselves.
Consequently, objects of charity become opportunities to be prized and made the most of.
Charity organizations are supported both by well-
meaning sympathetic persons and by publicity-
purchasing persons and their press-agents.

Many an ambitious politician or social climber
finds it profitable to become a patron of some sup-
posedly deserving charity. Recently, some one
inquired into the methods of a New York charity
organization, and found that the sum paid in
salaries to the various officers of the society was
more than twice the amount actually expended
in charity. But those who donated the money
got what they paid for; the hangers-on of the
society got what they wanted, and thereby lessened the actual harm that the money would have
done had it all reached its supposed objects.

While a limited amount of well-directed charitable effort may be for the general good, still by
far the larger part of promiscuous charity does
harm. Broadly speaking, charity of all kinds is
wrong in principle, because the misfortunes of

the unfit are a part of natural processes for their elimination, and anything done by charity to defeat the decrees of Nature is wrong.

These are some of the responsibilities for which we friends of peace must stand, if we succeed in preventing war by preparedness against war.

Those who are advocating the abolition of armaments, and are thereby fostering war, have not this responsibility; for, if they are successful in what they are teaching and doing, the pretty constant warfare that will prevail among the great nations during the next century will cure much of the hypersentimentalism that finds expression in large degenerative charities; and these charities will be swept away under the tread of marching armies. Whereas, if we succeed, by our advocacy, in securing adequate armaments, and thereby maintain enduring peace, then nothing can prevent our great promiscuous charities from continuing to secure the survival of the unfit with the continuous pollution of the blood-stream of the race from their degenerate blood through intermarriage with normal persons.

The arrestation of the self-purifying processes of Nature which are intended to clarify the blood of the race, by breeding the unfit and turning them back upon the race, is like turning the sewage of a city into its water supply.

If all incompetents—the hopelessly diseased and degenerate—were to be exterminated, it would be a very good thing for the race. Such methods have actually been practised in the past. At one time, when ancient Babylon was besieged, all the aged and diseased were murdered; and in ancient Greece, deformed or diseased children were killed at birth. But the trouble with this method is that no men possessing the human qualities rendering them worthy of survival could be found among us to do the wholesale executions. The mere possession of the inhuman qualities necessary to carry out the wholesale slaughter would elect the executioners themselves for slaughter. Man cannot be pitiless, like Nature, without himself becoming unworthy of pity, and, consequently, unworthy of survival.

Human survival must be co-operative. Human reproduction depends somewhat on lovability. According to the law of natural selection, a lovable person is selected rather than an unlovable person. Neither sex is so apt to fall in love and mate with a person of the other sex who is pitiless, as with one possessing pity and sympathy. Pity and sympathy, just like the love of parenthood, are bonds of the family. A community—a nation —is only a larger family.

Charity and sympathy make men gregarious. A world without charity or sympathy would be most unattractive. Human companionship in its higher values would not exist.

Nevertheless, when charity and sympathy build

and support large almshouses, until, as in London, one-third of all the property tax goes to the poor fund, then charity becomes an institution for breeding paupers and imbeciles. Such charity is the misuse of a virtue. Nine-tenths of all the paupers of one generation in England are children of the paupers of a preceding generation.

The following is what an eminent Englishman has to say of the condition of things in his country:

"We have a standing army of 1,200,000 paupers, and our permanent and occasional paupers number together at least 3,000,000. Our paupers are maintained at a yearly cost of about £30,000,000 to the community, and were it not for the Draconic administration of our poor-laws all our workhouses would be overcrowded by workers who would gladly exchange freedom and starvation wages for the confinement of the workhouse. No other nation has an army of paupers similar to that of Great Britain."—J. Ellis Barker, in *"Great and Greater Britain."*

A Cat Story

Once upon a time there was an excellent Queen who ruled over a beautiful and fruitful island. The island was not large; it had an area of only a few square miles, and the inhabitants numbered but a thousand. They lived mainly by fishing and agriculture.

The Queen loved both her people and her cats. As she would not allow a kitten killed, cats soon overran the palace. Some of these cats, dominated by the mousing instinct, took up their habitation in the fields and woods; for mice, small birds, squirrels, and all manner of cat-game were plentiful on the island.

The cats continued to multiply, until they became a great pest to the farmers, killing their chickens, ducklings, and song-birds. Then the good Queen divided the island between her people and her cats. She gave a tenth of the island to the cats. A fence was built between the cats and the people.

The cats soon multiplied to the number of 20,000, but there was not forage enough to feed them through the next winter; consequently, half of them died during the cold weather. In the autumn of the following year there were again 20,000 cats on the island, half of which were doomed to die by starvation during the winter; but the kind-hearted Queen taxed the people for food sufficient to feed the cats, and to save as many lives as possible.

The succeeding summer being long and fruitful, the cats thrived well, and the next autumn there were 50,000 cats on the island, and as there was but forage enough to winter 10,000 cats, 40,000 must starve during the coming winter, unless fed. Again the Queen taxed her people, and the cats were saved; but, to the amazement of the Queen and her little people, the next autumn brought 100,000 hungry cats to be fed, and it had come to a point where either the people or the cats must starve.

With grief, the Queen decided in favor of the people, for it was evident that, if the people were allowed to starve to save the cats, the cats also would starve without the people. That year, 90,000 cats starved to death on the island.

Thus, the good Queen's well-meant charity, intended to save 10,000 cats from starving to death, finally resulted in 90,000 cats starving to death. Actually, her attempt to lessen cat misery multiplied that misery nine-fold.

Now, what was true of those cats applies with exactly equal truth to the rearing of paupers and incompetents in times of peace.

In all the countries of the civilized world today, there are institutions for rearing and educating idiots. Sometimes, a section of an idiot's skull is cut out, and the skull trepanned in order to give his little brain room to expand. In this way, an idiot, incapable of feeding himself, may develop intelligence enough to vote, under the instruction of the ward-heeler, or he may even develop into a public expounder of the beauties of defenselessness as a safeguard against war.

The most common of all errors of conviction is the belief that knowledge of right-doing necessarily leads us to do right. But the truth is, that we are mainly guided by sentiment, even when it is diametrically opposed to our knowledge of right. No branch of our learning is more strongly fortified by facts of experience than that thoroughbred animals cannot be bred from scrub stock; that superior types of dogs cannot be bred from mongrels; that a fast trotting-horse is never sired by a Mexican burro or foaled by a heavy draughtmare.

We know absolutely that identically the same laws govern the breeding both of human beings and of the lower animals, and that exactly according to the seed sown will the fruit be. If sentiment leads us to sow tares among the wheat, we inevitably injure the wheat. No breeder of the lower animals would, from sentimental considerations, employ inferior types for his purposes.

With human growth, just as with the growth of vegetation in forest and field, there is only a certain limited amount of room in the sun, and a certain limited amount of nourishment and moisture in the soil. When charity aids an inferior type to secure a plot of earth and a plot of sky, it can do so only at the expense of some better type, which would otherwise have conquered the spaces

for itself, had not the inferior specimen had
charity as an ally.

Apropos of this philosophy, I quote the following from an article in *Science* by G. H. Parker,
Professor of Zoölogy, of Harvard:—

*"Thus asylums, retreats, hospitals, and so forth,
have been established by private munificence or
public grants. More or less under the protection of these institutions has grown up a body of
semi-dependents and defectives whose increase it
is that excites the apprehension of the eugenists.
That in the past such individuals have always
formed a part of our race cannot be doubted,
but that they ever showed a tendency to increase
comparable with what seems to be occurring at
present is highly improbable. The occasion of
this increase is not, in my opinion, merely the
exigencies of modern civilization; it is at least in
part due to the immense spread of humanitarian
activities which have characterized the last century of our civilization."*

If Andrew Carnegie were to give $100,000,000
for the support of paupers in the United States
and Great Britain, and another $100,000,000 for
the saving and kindly treatment and support of
imbeciles and incompetents, more continuous
harm to the race would result, by securing the
survival of the unfit, than would result from

a perpetual war between any two of the
nations now engaged in the great European
conflict.

As all charities thrive like a green bay tree in
times of peace, and are neglected in times of war,
it will be seen that charity alone in times of peace
is more potent in securing the survival of the
unfit than war could possibly be.

About here, the reader may conclude that I am
just as inconsistent in advocating armaments to
preserve peace, which, I hold, tends to foster degeneracy and decay, as are the pacifists who, by
advocating disarmament, promote war, which,
they hold, is most potential in fostering the same
thing.

But this is not so striking an inconsistency as
may first appear, because, as I have shown, nation-
wide military training, such as that practised in
Switzerland, would make for regeneracy and efficiency far more than all our charities, vices, and
profligacy make for degeneracy and decay. No
branch of education—not even all the prevalent
preachments on the subjects of hygiene, moral re-
form, cleanliness, temperance, and right living—
would be so influential for betterment as would the
introduction of the Swiss system of military training.

In order to be a good soldier, a man must be
fit, just as a college athlete must be fit; and military training, like the training of the college ath-

lete, compels him to observe the hygienic laws of right living.

We grow upon what we do and what we eat. If we live on an unbalanced food, which supplies too much of one kind of nourishment and too little of another, we become unbalanced in body and mind. Similarly, if our occupation exercises some of our organs and faculties too much and others not enough, we become unbalanced in body and mind.

The saying is trite that a sound mind requires a sound body. Likewise, a balanced mind must have a balanced body.

The occupations of civil life, if not constantly accompanied by systematic, scientific mental and physical training throw us out of balance. The success of Muldoon's famous human repair-shop depends entirely upon building up by proper food and strenuous exercise long-neglected organs and faculties.

The lower branches of a tree, which do not receive the necessary exercise from the wind, and the necessary vitalizing stimulus of the sun, gradually atrophy, and wither, die, and drop off; likewise do unused and unstimulated organs and faculties of the body shrink toward atrophy and pale toward death. The only part of a tree that is alive is where the sap runs. All the rest of the tree is dead. Organs and faculties of the human body not adequately exercised to circulate through

them the required amount of sap, gradually begin
to die.

Lord Kitchener is the Muldoon of the new English army. The raw recruits are trained for their
coming fight in much the same manner that a
pugilist is trained. They are made to take the
long walk out and the sharp run home, carrying
weights; they wrestle and spar; perform all manner of calisthenics and gymnastics; are fed proper
food, and are made properly to bathe. To the
great majority of them, this man-making training
is a revelation, but they find themselves so improved in health and so strengthened in body and
mind that, when they return to civil life, they
will still utilize much of the useful knowledge of
how to get fit and keep fit; and just as the hard
work imposed upon the soldiers is made easier by
their military training, so, when they return to
civil life, they will find all their tasks much easier
of accomplishment.

The following is quoted from a letter just received by me from a prominent English clergy-
man:

*"The war is making the Britisher a new man,
and he is blissfully unconscious of the conversion
in himself. Every class is feeling the uplift. He
will be stronger in his religion, his politics, and
his commerce. Half the men in Kitchener's Army
hate fighting and taking life. They have enlisted*

*for conscience' sake.   Naturally they will make
the finest soldiers."*

Soldierly fitness includes not only those sterling
qualities of higher manhood—cleanliness, temperance, efficiency, and moral stamina, raised from
a semi-subconscious latency into conscious action
by a military training—but also it includes that
very important attribute—devotion. A military
training develops a vague sense of patriotism
whose height is a hurrah for country, to that
height of devotion where one will gladly die for
his country.

In South America, there is a very potential
little republic where military training produces
just such beneficial results in a very high degree.
Chili, perhaps, comes nearer to Germany in economic efficiency than any other country in the
world.

Nothing could be more absurd than the fear of
the American people that a good-sized standing
army of trained soldiers would menace their liberty. The very preparation, by education and
training, necessary to make a good soldier, being
the very best training in the world to make him a
good citizen, would constitute one of the strongest fortifications possible to defend us against ourselves. It would act as a gyroscopic stabilizer
for our democratic institutions, and an equilibrator for our vacillating hot-air ship of state.

One of the very best books that I have yet seen upon the subject of peace and war is "Peace Insurance," by Richard Stockton, Jr., published in January, 1915, by A. C. McClurg and Company. It is a book that cannot fail at this time to do a large amount of good, and I heartily recommend it to the reader. I quote the following from its pages:

"To avoid exaggeration we shall quote first Mr. Kirkpatrick, who attempts to show the horrors of war in his book, 'War—What For?' by extracts from the New York Independent *of March 14, 1907:*

" 'It is the common consensus of opinion among investigators that industrial casualties in this nation number more than 500,000 yearly. Dr. Josiah Strong estimates the number at 564,000. As there are 525,600 minutes in a year, it may readily be seen that every minute (day and night) our industrial system sends to the graveyard or to the hospital a human being, the victim of some accident inseparable from his toil. We cry out against the horrors of war. . . . But the ravages . . . of industrial warfare are far greater than those of armed conflict. The number of killed or mortally wounded (including deaths from accidents, suicides, and murders, but excluding deaths from disease) in the Philippine War from February 4, 1899, to April 30, 1902, was 1,573. These

fatal casualties were spread over a period of three years and three months. But one coal mine alone in one year furnishes a mortality more than 38 per cent. in excess of this.

" 'The Japanese War is commonly looked upon as the bloodiest of modern wars. According to the official statement of the Japanese Government, 46,180 Japanese were killed, and 10,970 died of wounds. Our industrial war shows a greater mortality year by year.*

" 'But we are all of us more familiar with the Civil War, and we know what frightful devastation it caused in households North and South. It was, however, but a tame conflict compared with that which rages today, and which we call peace. The slaughter of its greatest battles are thrown in the shade by the slaughter which particular industries inflict today. Ask any schoolboy to name three of the bloodiest battles of that war, and he will probably name Gettysburg, Chancellorsville, and Chickamauga. The loss on both sides was:*

	Killed	Wounded
Gettysburg	*5,662*	*27,203*
Chancellorsville	*3,271*	*18,843*
Chickamauga	*3,924*	*23,362*
Total	*12,857*	*69,408*

" 'But our railroads, state and interstate, and our trolleys in one year equal this record in the* *number of killings and double it in the number of woundings.'*

"Said Dr. Josiah Strong in the North American Review for November, 1906:

" ' *We might carry on a half-dozen Philippine wars for three-quarters of a century with no larger number of total casualties than take place yearly in our peaceful industries.*

" '*Taking the lowest of our three estimates of industrial accidents, the total number of casualties suffered by our industrial army in one year is equal to the average annual casualties of our Civil War, plus those of the Philippine War, plus those of the Russian-Japanese War.*

" '*Think of carrying on three wars at the same time, world without end.*'

"Said President Roosevelt in his Annual Message for 1907:

" '*Industry in the United States now exacts . . . a far heavier toll of death than all of our wars put together. . . . The number of deaths in battle in all the foreign wars put together for the last century and a quarter, aggregate considerably less than one year's death record for our industries.*' . . .

"*Glancing over these comparisons between war and peace, we find that much of the horror of war dwindles away. Comparing those actually killed in industry and accident with those killed or dying from wounds in various wars, we find that the annual peace rate is approximately two and a half times that of the average annual Japanese loss, three times that of the Union loss in the Civil War, five times the Russian loss in the Japanese War, six times the Confederate loss in the Civil War, twenty-eight times the English loss in the Anglo-Boer War, and ninety times the American loss in the Spanish War. In other words, it would take the average annual deaths of the English and French in the Crimea, the Americans in the Mexican War, the North in the Civil War, the Americans in the Spanish War, the English in the Boer War, and the Japanese in the Russian War to approach the annual United States peace rate. Assuming the burden of all these wars, at once, and without ceasing, would be no more a drain than our peace death rate! Need we say more as to the cost in lives, as to the sorrowing mother, sweetheart, and wife? Think of these things. Where now is the bestiality and horror? Does it belong more to war where comparatively few die for their country willingly and nobly, or to peace where the multitudes die for sordid gain—for dollars and cents? Would it not be meet for the pacifists, assuming that they have*

*the best interest of the country at heart, to turn
first to the horrors of peace, and lastly to the horrors of war?"*

It is well to observe that a very large percentage
of the injuries and deaths in the United States in
times of peace, noted by Dr. Strong, are due to
preventable causes, and one of the best remedies is
a military training. In Germany, the number of
persons per capita of population killed and injured by accidents in time of peace is not half as
great as it is in the United States.

These losses are part of the high price that this
country pays for inefficiency. They could be very
largely remedied by military training, which
quickens awareness and alertness. Many an accident resulting in severe wounding or death is due
to undeveloped and untrained powers of mind, and
to lack of physical co-ordination. In the works
of the National Cash Register Company, at Day-
ton, Ohio, where all employees are given the
equivalent of military training in care and efficiency, personal injury through accidents is almost entirely eliminated.

A man who has been taught to play football and
to box and wrestle in his youth is not nearly so
likely in after years to fall and injure himself,
or to be hit by a trolley car, or automobile, as
one who has not had that training. Similarly, a
man who, in his youth, has had his mind developed

to quick alertness, and every muscle of his body brought under the domination of the will by military training, is far less likely to be injured by accident than one who has not had a military training. Consequently, many of the ills of peace may be cured by the practice of the very medicine that is the best remedy for war.

William James, in an article entitled, "The Moral Equivalent of War," starts out with the remark, "The war against war is going to be no holiday excursion or camping party." He adds that, "There is something highly paradoxical in the modern man's relation to war."

He continues:

"Ask all our millions north and south whether they would vote now to have our war for the Union expunged from history, and the record of a peaceful transition to the present time substituted for that of its marches and battles, and, probably hardly a handful of eccentrics would say yes.

"Yet ask those same people whether they would be willing in cold blood to stand another civil war now to gain another similar possession, and not one man or woman would vote for the proposition."

Let us suppose that the same Southern states that then seceded were to secede again today, capture all the negroes there and all men and women whose skins are tinted by negro blood, enslave them, and establish anew the auction block at the slave market: then let us ask the people of the North Mr. James's second question.

What defense has the average person against being convinced by such sophistry, coming from so eminent a psychologist and philosopher as William James? The conclusion of the average person is: "A great man like him must know better than I, he having made a study of such things." This article was given wide circulation by the Association for International Conciliation. It was also published in *McClure's Magazine,* and again in the *Popular Science Monthly.*

Others have said, and are saying, similar silly things about the war against war, but they are not men of such intellectual eminence as was William James. It is true that Dr. David Starr Jordan is a very prominent person, and says things even sillier than anything that William James said, but exactly there is the saving grace of his sayings. Some of his conclusions are so utterly irrational and absurd as to enable a very large number of persons to perceive their falsity, whereas the error is not so easily perceived in such statements as the foregoing quoted from Mr. James.

Let us examine the proposition to make war on war. The only common-sense way to wage war on war is to war against the evils that produce war. To wage war on war, which comes like the visitation of a physician, to cure ills, would be like waging war on the medical profession to cure a decimating pestilence. To arrest the hand of the surgeon in order to save bloodshed is to let the patient die of cancer.

Our Civil War was merely a great surgical operation which removed a malignant cancer from the breast of Columbia. Mars, the old and experienced surgeon, made a good job of it. Columbia's ailment was one that could not be cured by physic, poultice, incantations, or other quack nostrums, which, Mr. James suggested, might have been tried. The patient had to be operated on with the sword, so that the question as to the right or wrong of the Civil War, and as to whether it should have then been fought, and whether, if it had been delayed till now, it should now be fought, depends upon a choice of evils— depends entirely upon whether or not American slavery was a greater evil than the American Civil War.

Two of my brothers were killed in the awful struggle to free the slaves and save the Union. It was worth the price to them, to me, and to the rest of my family; and I am of the opinion that every other family in the country who made a like sacrifice would agree with me that to free four millions of human beings from bondage was worth the price. Emancipation then not only freed four millions, but it saved, between that time and now, more than twenty millions from the yoke and the lash. But, what is still more important, the emancipation of the slaves emancipated their masters also—emancipated all of us, North and South—and raised the proclamation of human equality by our country's fathers from a mockery and a shame to a reality.

If there were men and women and children bought and sold in this country today, you and I, reader, would mix up in the infamous business with gun and sword, and we would not wait long to do much voting about it, either. "Great national problems," said Bismarck, "are solved not by speeches and resolutions of majorities, but by blood and iron."

It is very evident that it would have been wrong in 1860 for some powerful external force, waging war against war, to have prevented the Civil War, and thereby have prevented the emancipation of the slaves.

It is all very well at this time to prate about the possibility of a peaceful settlement of the differences between the North and South before the Civil War broke out. That is exactly what was tried. Even after the war broke out, Lincoln, one of the greatest men that America ever produced, tried with all his might to do that very thing. War was the only way.

A very large percentage of the wars of the

world have been waged for freedom—have been wars for justice, and against tyranny. To war against such wars would be to war for tyranny, and against freedom and justice. Actually, those who today are recruiting for the war against war are asking you to enlist in a campaign to shackle the hands of the oppressed in future years, and tie them down with ball and chain to prevent them from striking for liberty. They are to be denied the right of war for freedom, which was our right in the Revolution.

Every man exerts a positive influence either for good or for evil. If the advocates of disarmament and non-resistance are exerting a good influence, then I am exerting a bad influence, and every advocate of armed defense is a worker of evil. You, reader, must judge between us.

If it is wrong to insure with armaments against invasion of this country, which invasion would mean the violation of our homes, the rape of our wives and daughters and sisters and sweethearts; if it is right to invite invasion by non-resistance, and wrong to oppose it with force; if, when an enemy injures us, it is the correct thing to let him add insult to the first offense; then it is wrong to be a man, it is wrong to resent dishonor of the home, and all of us who have any manhood in us should be emasculated.

If, when this country is invaded, some militant scoundrel, forcing his way into your home, should lay the hand of violent lust on trembling wife or daughter, would you observe the pacifist policy of non-resistance, or would you kill him right there, even if it cost you your life? I know your answer. The invading army would be lessened by one soldier, or there would be one less American.

CONCLUSION

WHAT SHALL THE END BE?

IS it possible to prescribe a remedy for war? We know that law, unsupported by force, cannot be substituted for war. We know that war will obey no law other than that of necessity, and, consequently, that the settling of national differences at an international court of conciliatory arbitration is not workable. We know that no nation will abide by the dictates of any such court when those dictates are opposed to its interests, unless that court has the power to enforce its decrees.

We know, then, that an international court of arbitration can dispense only such justice as may be consistent with the interests and necessities of the nations possessing the power to dominate that court; therefore, we know that the greatest measure of justice and the greatest security for peace that may be expected are only what may be pledged by the union of a majority of the great nations in a pool of their national interests and necessities, to maintain such international order as shall be consistent with the terms of the pool.

[306]

All other nations outside of the pool will then be compelled to observe the law of the pooling nations, because the necessity of keeping peace with these dominant Powers will be greater than any other necessity.

The justice that the weaker nations may expect will depend upon the degree in which their individual interests are the mutual concern of the larger interests.

Armies and navies will then become veritable international police forces, and the necessity for large competitive armaments will be very greatly lessened.

There will then be greater security for peace, although this striving world is not likely soon to be a safe and quiet nesting place for the dove of peace; because at any time, when the necessities of the pooling nations shall put too great a strain on the compact, then the pool will break and war ensue. The great aim of the peoples of the nations should not be for a Utopian peace based on merely sentimental grounds, but for a peace secured by so practicable an *entente* and pact between the great Powers as shall, entirely aside from sentiment, work for the best welfare of the world.

Russian, Teuton, Frenchman, Anglo-Saxon, when you shall have returned your blood-wet swords to their scabbards, then join hands overseas with us Americans, who are kin to all the blood you have spilled, and let us take serious counsel of one another.

But, Americans, though we may turn our face toward the morning that should come, such posturing cannot, any more than the cock's-crow, bring the morning; and until the great international compact be made, we shall be able to find safety only by adequate preparation to stand alone against the dread eventuality of war.

INDEX

INDEX

[311]

INDEX

Balloon, developed with aëro-plane, 204;
modern, 205;
dirigible, has one advantage over aëroplane, 210.

Battle-cruiser, modern, absence of any in U. S., 188; adopted by foreign countries, 188.

Beatty, Admiral, reports on North Sea fight, 195.

Belgian women, abject condition of, 244, 245.

Bernhardi, extracts from his "How Germany Makes War," 89.

Bessemer steel process introduced by Carnegie, 252.

Bethlehem Steel Company, manufacture of guns and armor-plate, 9, 10, 76.

Billings, Josh, on ignorance, 23.

Bismarck, 163.

Blatchford, Robert, writer for *The Daily Mail*, quoted, 164-67;
mentioned, 167.

Bliss, E. W., Torpedo Works, 77.

Bloch, M. de, author of "The Future of War," against possibility of war, 2;
discussed, 93, 95.

Bluecher, the, 187.

Bombshells, 185;
dropped from airship not very effective, 209.

"Britannia Rules the Waves," 97.

Buckner, Colonel E. G., vice-president of du Pont Powder Company, 257.

Buffington, General A. R., 200, 201.

Cæsar, massacres by, 40;
mentioned, 90, 162.

Can Law Be Substituted for War? Chapter II, 22.

Canal, Panama, 157, 173.

Canning, George, attempts to join England in her open-door policy, 58.

Cannon designed by Mr. Maxim to illustrate advantages of projectiles of great size, 198;
description of, 198, 199.

Carlyle, quotations from, 49.

Carnegie, Andrew, 68, 290;
his ideas on military defenselessness, 69;
quotation from, 70-71;
his views discussed, 71, 72, 73, 74, 75, 78, 80;
greatest American armorer, 252.

Chaffee, Lieut.-Gen. Adna R., quotation from, 68.

Charity, evils of, 283, 284, 285, 289;
J. Ellis Barker on, 286;
cat story illustrating evils of mistaken, 286-88;
thrives in time of peace, forgotten in times of war, 291.

Chittenden, Hiram M., his arraignment of war, 267-68.

Christian Herald, The, 46.

Colt Patent Firearms, 76.

Congress, dependent upon will of people, 132-33;
has power to dominate Army and Navy, 141;
not qualified to pass judgment on Army and Navy, 144;
neglects to take necessary precautions against war, 145;
decides strength of Navy, 164;
and the General Board, 168.

Conscription, values of, 136;
enforced in Germany, 136.

INDEX

INDEX

INDEX

[315]

INDEX

INDEX

INDEX

PRAISE FROM PATRIOTS

Extracts From a Few of Hundreds of Letters Praising
HUDSON MAXIM'S DEFENSELESS AMERICA

THEODORE ROOSEVELT:

" 'Defenseless America' is a capital book. I hope it
will have the widest possible circulation throughout
our country. The prime duty for this nation is to
prepare itself so that it can protect itself; and this is
the duty that you are preaching in your admirable
volume."

OSCAR S. STRAUS:

" 'Defenseless America', coming from an expert, will
awaken interest in the most practical method of securing peace by safeguarding our national existence.
I am in fullest accord with your Conclusion—an international compact with adequate international force
to maintain it, and give adequate guarantee to enforce
its decrees."

S. S. McCLURE:

"A most convincing book on an extraordinarily important subject, done in a manner not only convincing
but irrefutable."

REAR-ADMIRAL CHARLES D. SIGSBEE:

"I should not have said that the subject could be
treated in a way to make it fascinating to the popular
reader, yet I now think that is precisely what you
have done. May the book bear good fruit!"

GARRETT P. SERVISS:

" 'Defenseless America' ought to go into the hands
of ten million American citizens before another month
passes. You have done a magnificent thing for your
country! In God's name, may she turn from the silly
twaddle of the pacifist wiseacres, and save herself,
even on the crumbling verge!"

[319]

PRAISE FROM PATRIOTS

GEORGE VON LENGERKE MEYER:

"It will go a great ways toward aiding the people of this country to realize the necessity of a proper national defense and a preparedness against war."

MRS. JOHN A. LOGAN:

"I wish that every official in the land could read it."

DR. ORISON SWETT MARDEN:

"A colossal, monumental treatment of the subject."

FRANKLIN D. ROOSEVELT:

"You have brought the whole question of National Defense to a basis which can be readily understood by the average layman."

LIEUT. BARON HROLF VON DEWITZ:

"In 'Defenseless America' you explode a crater of information on the subject such as has never been detonated before."

COL. BEVERLEY W. DUNN:

"I wish to congratulate you on the conspicuous and valuable service that you have rendered the people of the United States in writing this book."

DR. E. C. BECK:

"I want to thank you from the bottom of my heart for this masterpiece of revelation on your part, this opus which I look upon in the nature of an historical event. May the Lord use your book to pound a little sense into our fellow citizens."

REV. J. F. STILLEMANS:

"I am only one of thousands who would welcome an edition as cheap as possible of 'Defenseless America' so that we could distribute it freely."

CLEVELAND MOFFETT:

" 'Defenseless America' is great stuff and ought to be read by every loyal American."

W. SIDNEY JOPSON:

"The direct results of reading 'Defenseless America' were that I went to Plattsburg and applied for admission in our National Guard."

PRAISE FROM EDITORS

No Serious Book Has Ever Been More Highly Praised by
the Leading Newspapers of America.

PHILADELPHIA PUBLIC LEDGER:

"A book by an expert in modern armament who
writes with graphic power what he knows better than
anyone in this country—a solemn warning."

NEW YORK AMERICAN:

"No book issued on the subject marshals with equal
skill so great an array of facts as Mr. Maxim's volume.
In the present state of national thought upon our military and naval needs this book is most valuable."

WASHINGTON STAR:

"In origin and treatment this is a surpassing study
whose sheer information, apart from its personal conclusions, is worth the serious attention, not only of the
legislator, but of the plain man behind the lawmaker."

DETROIT FREE PRESS:

"Hudson Maxim makes a call to arms against war.
Here is an argument for proper armament from a
man who not only foretold the Japanese war and
named the victor, but also prophesied the present conflict and by knowledge and study of world's conditions
knows what he is talking about and makes his warning timely."

LOS ANGELES TIMES:

"A powerful book on an imminent and national
problem that every thinking citizen should read with
care."

BOSTON TRANSCRIPT:

"Shows how it is safer for a country like the United
States with so large a territory to defend, to prepare,
so that no foreign nation will be anxious to try a struggle with us. The peace of the United States will then
rest on a firm foundation."

PRAISE FROM EDITORS

BALTIMORE SUN:

"The book is brilliantly written, with the severity of one who intensely desires to drive a truth home and with the assurance of one who feels his statistics unassailable and his arguments unanswerable. He is supported by many witnesses whose knowledge must be respected. There is no smallness in the writer's attitude. He appears to feel intensely his mission as prophet and patriot."

CLEVELAND PLAIN DEALER:

"Here is a man, frankly interested in war, who seems utterly honest in his beliefs. The book contains an expert elucidation of the weaknesses of the American army and navy. It has practical suggestions for improvement. It is, in fact, a complete text book for the student of American preparedness or unpreparedness, written, of course, in a sincerely ex parte manner."

BROOKLYN CITIZEN:

"The book should be read and studied carefully by every lover of his country."

LEWISTON JOURNAL:

" 'Defenseless America' is a ringing and insistent call, calculated to startle the average American out of his peaceful and complacent sense of security."

NEW YORK PRESS:

"The book is interesting—as interesting as a well-written and absorbing novel, only it deals with vital facts that have a bearing on the lives and fortunes of every one in this country."

THE OUTLOOK:

"We wish that we could think that those who are opposed to any preparation against war by this country would read and consider this book of Mr. Hudson Maxim."

LIFE, N. Y.:

"One of the early lumber-camp tales ended with a stirring scene in which a big, sandy-haired hero, caught in the path of a bursting log jam, hurls his cap defiantly into the advancing wall of destruction, just before it whelms him. Such a gesture, futile yet magnificent, is suggested by Hudson Maxim's fiery appeal to the sleeping intelligence and lulled self-interest of his countrymen, 'Defenseless America.' The book contains a remorseless marshaling of stern facts, fused into prophecy by a sort of incandescent logic. It is the first bold proclaiming of the bitter 'civilization' truths revealed by the vast disillusionment of the war. And these are here flung, as the author feels, into the face of approaching national disaster."

THE SCIENTIFIC AMERICAN:

"The scope of 'Defenseless America' is so all-embracing, that the author has given a veritable mine of information upon the subject of war and war material. Mr. Maxim is well qualified by his long and successful association, as a practical and successful inventor, with the production of the implements of war, to write upon the technical side of the question; and this he does with a characteristic force and lucidity which will render the subject perfectly understandable and full of fascinating interest for the average layman."

REVIEW OF REVIEWS:

"A graphic and effective presentation of facts revealing the defenseless condition of this country and indicating what must be done to avert national humiliation."

———

"THIS POWERFUL BOOK HAS JARRED
AMERICAN COMPLACENCY AS NO
OTHER BOOK HAS EVER
DONE"

———

From The New York American

———

One of the most remarkable men of our time has written a book—and the book is probably the most startling document ever placed before the American people. Its author is Hudson Maxim, world-famous inventor, writer on many topics of public interest, member of the Naval Advisory Board—and an American patriot.

His book, called "Defenseless America," has fallen among the complacent, the self-satisfied, the careless and the indifferent like a seventeen-inch shell.

[323]

It is a pitiless book—pitiless in its facts, pitiless in its logic, pitiless in its conclusions.

Mr. Maxim knows what he is writing about; he is one of the greatest authorities on military affairs in the world. His book has the cold steel precision of truth.

He shows that all wars have economic causes, no matter how they are painted over with sentiment. And he demonstrates that one of the most urgent economic incentives to war that has ever existed will be the relative condition of Europe and the United States at the close of the Great War.

Imagine the victors of this gigantic conflict—Allies or Teutons—impoverished in money and resources, with the most colossal public debt in the world's history hanging over them, but possessing an enormous army of trained veterans and a world-beating navy.

Then, on this side of the Atlantic, a nation that thinks it "can whip all creation," and acts on that principle—a hundred million over-fed, money-making people, nine-tenths of whom could not load a modern infantry rifle if they should ever happen to see one; a country of countless dollars protected by obsolete battleships and submarines that can neither float nor sink; a nation rich but undefended, confident but weak, dictatorial in manner but powerless in action.

America sits on an open powder barrel. Will the Victors of the Great War apply the match?

Get this stirring and tremendous book, and read what will happen—in Mr. Maxim's own words. He will tell you where the match will be applied, what points in controversy will bring on the collision—and then what will take place with startling swiftness.

And—

He tells what may be done, even at this late day, for effective defense.

As Mr. Maxim has cut out all royalty, the publishers are thereby enabled to furnish a special edition of the book, of which this volume is a sample, at only fifty cents a copy.

The book may be obtained of or ordered through any bookstore, or the publishers, Hearst's International Library Company, 119 West 40th Street, New York, will send it postage paid to any address for sixty cents, or ten copies in a single package for five dollars—fifty cents a copy. The library edition, superior paper and binding, may still be had at two dollars a copy.